modern country knits

30 DESIGNS FROM JUNIPER MOON FARM / SUSAN GIBBS

sixth&springbooks
NEW YORK

161 AVENUE OF THE AMERICAS,
NEW YORK, NY 10013
sixthandspringbooks.com

Editorial Director: JOY AQUILINO

Managing Editors:
KRISTY MCGOWAN
LAURA COOKE

Senior Editor: LISA SILVERMAN

Art Director: DIANE LAMPHRON

Page Design: MICHELLE HENNING

Yarn Editor: VANESSA PUTT

Editorial Assistant: JOHANNA LEVY

Supervising Patterns Editor:
LORI STEINBERG

Patterns Editors:
PAT HARSTE, RENEE LORION,
MARI LYNN PATRICK,
MARGEAU SOBOTI

Technical Illustrations:
LORETTA DACHMAN

Photography: SUSAN GIBBS

Fashion Styling:
SUSAN GIBBS, LAURIA KINCAID

Hair & Makeup: LAURIA KINCAID

Vice President: TRISHA MALCOLM

Publisher: CAROLINE KILMER

Production Manager:
DAVID JOINNIDES

President: ART JOINNIDES

Chairman: JAY STEIN

Copyright © 2014 by Susan Gibbs

Library of Congress Cataloging-in-Publication Data
Gibbs, Susan (Farmer)
Modern country knits : 30 designs from Juniper Moon Farm / Susan Gibbs.
    pages cm
 ISBN 978-1-936096-79-4
1. Knitting—Patterns. I. Title.
TT825.G5155 2014
746.43'2—dc23

2014010932

MANUFACTURED IN CHINA

1 3 5 7 9 10 8 6 4 2

First Edition

For my mother and sister,
who always knew I could.
And for Mike,
who made sure I did.

paducah pullover
page 92

contents

INTRODUCTION 7

Abilene Stole 10

Dyer Brook Blouse 14

Mattatuck Tee 20

Sheridan Shawl 24

Darlington Dress 27

Silverton Top and Cowl 32

Cody Hat and Cowl 38

Carroll Cardigan 42

Fayette Stole 48

Traverse City Tunic 51

Edgewater Shawl 56

Maryville Cardigan 60

Williston Hat 66

Spring Hill Scarf 69

County Line Vest 72

Hopewell Hat and Mitts 76

Cloudcroft Pullover 82

Summerdale Dress 85

Brandywine Stole 89

Paducah Pullover 92

Oak Harbor Pullover 97

Bedford Shawl 101

River Falls Cardigan 104

Pella Pullover 110

Quinby Capelet 116

Meadow Vale Mitts 119

Pebble Creek Pullover 122

Rock Springs Wrap 126

Ashland Pullover 128

Decorah Cardigan 132

dyer brook blouse
page 14

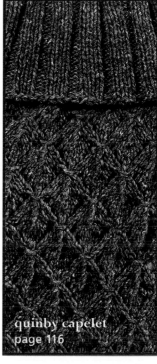

quinby capelet
page 116

ABOUT THE YARNS 138

TIPS & TOOLS 139

ACKNOWLEDGMENTS 143

INDEX 144

williston hat
page 66

maryville cardigan
page 60

edgewater shawl
page 56

introduction

The story of Juniper Moon Farm will sound familiar to anyone who has ever picked up a pair of knitting needles: girl learns to knit and immediately fantasizes about owning a flock of sheep.

What made my story different? My life was in a place where running away to start a farm was actually doable. I had recently left my job as a network news producer in search of a more authentic life. I pictured myself knitting in the pasture, surrounded by gamboling lambs, classical music in the background. It was a lovely dream, and one that I couldn't resist turning into a reality.

Of course, the reality was nothing like the fantasy. Shepherding is hard, dirty, sometimes heartbreaking work—but it was also more fulfilling than I could have imagined. Watching a newborn lamb take its first shaky steps on impossibly long legs is magical, even without the soundtrack.

With all that hard work and a lot of luck, the demand for Juniper Moon Farm's yarns quickly outgrew my flock's production. I started creating yarns using wool, alpaca, silk, and cotton grown by farmers all over the world. Today, those yarns are available in shops all over the U.S. and Canada.

One of the most fun parts of running Juniper Moon Farm is working with talented and creative knitwear designers, who over the years have worked with our yarns and helped define the JMF aesthetic: feminine but not girly, with a focus on wearability and attention to detail.

The projects in this book perfectly capture that spirit. From the elegance of Melissa Leapman's Silverton Top and Cowl, to the preppy look of Theresa Schabes's County Line Vest, to the whimsy of Nadia Elgawarsha's Williston Hat, you'll find modern but classic pieces for every style and skill level. I know you'll love knitting them with the beautiful yarns that are the products of my fantasy-turned-reality. ✳

the projects

abilene stole

DESIGNED BY
YOKO HATTA
■■■■

Traditional Shetland lace becomes a truly ethereal experience in a delicate and versatile rectangular wrap.

FINISHED MEASUREMENTS
Approximately 15 x 66"/38 x 167.5cm

YARN & NOTIONS
1 ball *Findley* in color #14 Dove

US 4 (3.5mm) straight needles *or size used to obtain gauge*

GAUGE
Approx 20 sts and 25 rows = 4"/10cm in chart 3 after blocking with size US 4 (3.5mm) needles. *Take time to check your gauge.*

GLOSSARY
BORDER PATTERN
(multiple of 12 sts plus 1)
ROW 1 (RS) K1, *[k2tog] twice, [yo, k1] 3 times, yo, [SKP] twice, k1; rep from * to end.
ROW 2 Knit.
Rep rows 1 and 2 for border pat.

SHAWL
Cast on 75 sts loosely, placing markers after first 7 sts and before last 7 sts.
Knit 2 rows.

BEGIN CHARTS AND BORDER PAT
NEXT ROW (RS) Work row 1 of chart 1 to marker, sl marker, work row 1 of border pat to marker, sl marker, work row 1 of chart 2 over 7 sts.
NEXT ROW (WS) Work row 2 of chart 2 to marker, sl marker, work border pat to marker, sl marker, work row 2 of chart 1 to end.
Cont in this way until chart row 12 is complete.

BEGIN CHART 3
NEXT ROW (RS) Work row 1 of chart 1 to marker, sl marker, k to rep line of chart 3, work 6-st rep 8 times across, work to end of chart 3, sl marker, work row 1 of chart 2 to end.
Cont to foll charts in this way until row 4 of chart 3 is complete. Then rep rows 1–12 of charts 1 and 2 and rows 1–4 of chart 3 until piece measures approx 64"/164cm from beg, end with a row 12 of charts 1 and 2.

BORDER
NEXT ROW (RS) Work row 1 of chart 1 to marker, sl marker, k to next marker, sl marker, work row 1 of chart 2 to end.
Knit 1 row.
NEXT ROW (RS) Work row 3 of chart 1 to marker, sl marker, work border pat to marker, sl marker, work row 3 of chart 2 to end.
Cont to foll charts in this way until chart row 11 is complete. Bind off loosely.

FINISHING
Block to open lace, pinning out points of edges and borders. ✳

abilene stole

CHART 1

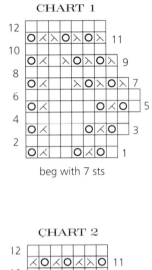

beg with 7 sts

CHART 2

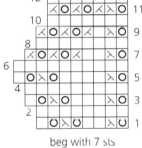

beg with 7 sts

CHART 3

6-st rep

Stitch Key

☐	k on RS, p on WS	◿	k2tog
—	p on RS, k on WS	◺	SKP
☐ yo		◮	sssk

dyer brook blouse

DESIGNED BY
CAROLINE FRYAR
■■□□

A tonal yarn adds
subtle depth to
a textured lacy top.

SIZES
XS (S, M, L, 1X)
Shown in XS.

FINISHED MEASUREMENTS
BUST 33 (36½, 40, 43, 45)"/83(91,
99, 107, 113)cm
LENGTH 20 (20½, 21, 21½, 22)"/51
(52, 53.5, 54.5, 56)cm
UPPER ARM 13 (13, 13½, 13½,
14)"/33 (33, 34.5, 34.5, 35.5)cm

YARN & NOTIONS
2 balls *Findley Dappled*
in color #06 Driftwood

US 3 (3.25mm) circular needles,
16 and 24"/40 and 60cm long, and
straight needles, *or size used to
obtain gauge*

Stitch markers

GAUGES
20 sts and 32 rows = 4"/10cm
after blocking in St st with
US 3 (3.25mm) needles.

24 sts and 37 rows = 4"/10cm after
blocking in chart C pat with
US 3 (3.25mm) needles.
Take time to check your gauges.

GLOSSARY
MAKE NUPP Into same st, work ([k1, yo] twice, k1)—5 sts.
GATHER 5 K5tog but do not sl from LH needle, [yo, k same 5 sts tog without slipping from needle] twice, sl all 5 sts to RH needle.

NOTES
1) When working shaping in lace patterns when there are no longer enough sts to work a yarn over inc with its corresponding decrease, work those sts in St st.
2) Sweater is designed to be worn with 0"/0cm ease.

BACK
Cast on 97 (105, 113, 121, 127) sts using a stretchy cast-on, such as the Norwegian long-tail cast-on, or cast on using a larger needle.
NEXT ROW (WS) Sl 1, p to end.

BEGIN CHARTS C AND B
NEXT ROW (RS) Sl 1, k5 (9, 13, 17, 20), place marker (pm), work row 1 of chart C to rep line, work 12-st rep twice, work to end of chart, pm, work row 1 of chart B over next 19 sts, pm, work row 1 of chart C to rep line, work 12-st rep twice, work to end of chart, pm, k to end.
Cont to work charts in this way, slipping first st of each row and working sts outside chart pats in St st, slipping markers every row. Rep rows 1–12 of chart C and rows 1 40 of chart B to end, AT THE SAME TIME, when row 7 is complete, shape waist as foll:

SHAPE WAIST
NEXT (DEC) ROW (RS) Sl 1, k2tog, work in pats as established to last 3 sts, ssk, k1—2 sts dec'd.
Cont in pats as established, rep dec row every 8th row 3 times more—89 (97, 105, 113, 119) sts.
Work even for 23 rows more.
NEXT (INC) ROW (RS) Sl 1, M1, work to last st, M1, k1.
Cont in pats as established, rep inc row every 24th row once more—93 (101, 109, 117, 123) sts.
Work even in pats until piece measures 12 (12¼, 12½, 12¾, 13)"/30.5 (31, 31.5, 32.5, 33)cm from beg, end with a WS row.

SHAPE ARMHOLE
NOTE When there are no longer enough sts to work an inc with

dyer brook blouse

its corresponding dec, work those sts in St st.

Bind off 3 (4, 5, 6, 7) sts at beg of next 2 rows—87 (93, 99, 105, 109) sts.

NEXT (DEC) ROW (RS) Sl 1, k2tog, work to last 3 sts, ssk, k1—2 sts dec'd.

NEXT (DEC) ROW (WS) Sl 1, p2tog tbl, work to last 3 sts, p2tog, p1—2 sts dec'd.

Rep last 2 rows 3 times more—71 (77, 83, 89, 93) sts.

Cont in pats as established until armhole measures 6 (6¼, 6¼, 6½, 6½)"/15 (15.5, 15.5, 16, 16)cm, end with a WS row.

SHAPE NECK

NEXT ROW (RS) Work 27 (29, 31, 34, 35) sts in pats as established; with a 2nd ball of yarn, bind off center 17 (19, 21, 21, 23) sts, work to end of row.

Working each side at once with a separate ball of yarn, bind off 6 sts from each neck edge twice—16 (18, 20, 23, 24) sts rem for each shoulder.

Cont in pat until armhole measures 7 (7¼, 7½, 7¾, 8)"/18 (18.5, 19, 19.5, 20.5)cm. Bind off.

FRONT

Cast on 95 (103, 111, 119, 125) sts.

NEXT ROW (WS) Sl 1, p to end.

BEGIN CHARTS A AND B

NEXT ROW (RS) Sl 1, k10 (14, 18, 22, 25) sts, pm, work row 1 of chart A over next 27 sts, pm, work row 1 of chart B over next 19 sts, pm, work row 1 of chart A over next 27 sts, pm, k to end.

Cont to work charts in this way, slipping first st of each row and working sts outside chart pats in St st, slipping markers every row. Rep rows 1–16 of chart A and rows 1–40 of chart B to end, AT THE SAME TIME, when row 7 is complete, shape waist as foll:

SHAPE WAIST

NEXT (DEC) ROW (RS) Sl 1, k2tog, work to last 3 sts, ssk, k1—2 sts dec'd.

Cont in pats as established, rep dec row every 8th row 3 times more—87 (95, 103, 111, 117) sts.

Work even for 23 rows more.

NEXT (INC) ROW (RS) Sl 1, M1, work to last st, M1, k1.

Cont in pats as established, rep inc row every 24th row once more—91 (99, 107, 115, 121) sts.

Work even until piece measures same as back to armholes, end with a WS row.

SHAPE ARMHOLES

Bind off 3 (4, 5, 6, 7) sts at beg of next 2 rows—85 (91, 97, 103, 107) sts.

NEXT (DEC) ROW (RS) Sl 1, k2tog, work to last 3 sts, ssk, k1—2 sts dec'd.

NEXT (DEC) ROW (WS) Sl 1, p2tog tbl, work to last 3 sts, p2tog, p1—2 sts dec'd.

Rep last 2 rows 3 times more—69 (75, 81, 87, 91) sts.

Work even until armhole measures 4 (4¼, 4½, 4¾, 5)"/10 (11, 12, 11.5, 12.5)cm, end with a WS row.

SHAPE NECK

NEXT ROW (RS) Work 26 (28, 30, 33, 34) sts in pats as established, join a 2nd ball of yarn and bind off center 17 (19, 21, 21, 23) sts, work to end of row.

Working both sides at once with separate balls of yarn, bind off 4 sts from each neck edge once, 3 sts from each neck edge once, 2 sts from each neck edge once, and 1 st from each neck edge once—16 (18, 20, 23, 24) sts rem for each shoulder. Work even until armhole measures 7 (7¼, 7½, 7¾, 8)"/18 (18.5, 19, 19.5, 20.5)cm. Bind off.

SLEEVE

Cast on 71 (71, 73, 73, 75) sts.

Work in garter st for 1"/2.5cm, end with a WS row.

BEGIN CHART C

NEXT ROW (RS) Sl 1, k 0 (0, 1, 1, 2), pm, work row 1 of chart C to rep line, work 12-st rep 5 times across, work to end of chart, pm, k to end.

Cont to work charts in this way, slipping first st of each row and working sts outside chart pats in St st, slipping markers every row. Rep rows 1–12 of chart C to end, AT THE SAME TIME, when piece measures 3"/7.5cm from beg, end with a WS row, shape sleeve as foll:

SHAPE SLEEVE

NEXT (INC) ROW (RS) Sl 1, M1, work to last st, M1, k1—2 sts inc'd.

Cont in pat as established, rep inc row every 16th row 3 times more, then work 1 more WS row—79 (79, 81, 81, 83) sts.

dyer brook blouse

SHAPE CAP
Bind off 3 (4, 5, 6, 7) sts at beg of next 2 rows—73 (71, 71, 69, 69) sts.
NEXT (DEC) ROW (RS) Sl 1, k2tog, work to last 3 sts, ssk, k1—2 sts dec'd.
NEXT (DEC) ROW (WS) Sl 1, p2tog tbl, work to last 3 sts, p2tog, p1—2 sts dec'd.
Rep these 2 rows 3 (2, 2, 1, 1) times more—57 (59, 59, 61, 61) sts.
Work 8 rows even in pat as established.
NEXT (DEC) ROW (RS) Sl 1, k2tog, work to last 3 sts, ssk, k1—2 sts dec'd.
Rep RS dec row *every other* row 12 (12, 13, 13, 14) times more—31 (33, 31, 33, 31) sts.
Rep RS and WS dec rows as before *every* row 4 times more—15 (17, 15, 17, 15) sts. Bind off.

FINISHING
Block pieces to measurements. Sew shoulder seams. Set in sleeves. Sew sleeve and side seams.

LOWER BORDER
With longer circular needle, pick up and k 1 st for each of the sts along bottom edge. Pm for beg of rnd. Work in garter st for 1"/2.5cm. Bind off.

NECK BAND
With shorter circular needle, pick up and k 1 st for each of the bound-off sts along back neck and along front neck edge, and 2 sts for every 3 rows along the side neck edges. Pm for beg of rnd. Work in garter st for 1"/2.5cm. Bind off very loosely. ✳

CHART B

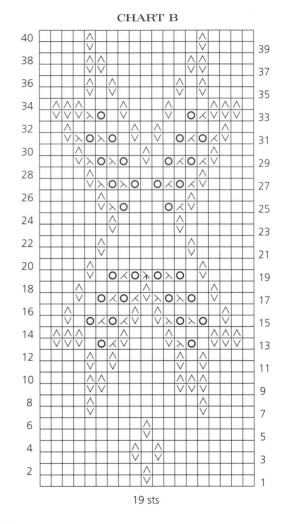

19 sts

CHART A

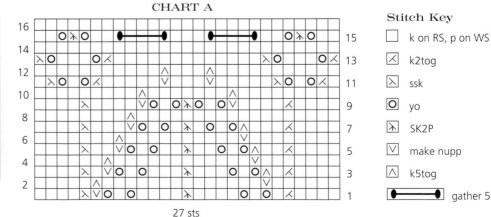

27 sts

Stitch Key

☐	k on RS, p on WS
⊼	k2tog
⊼	ssk
⊙	yo
⋏	SK2P
⋁	make nupp
⋀	k5tog
•▬•	gather 5

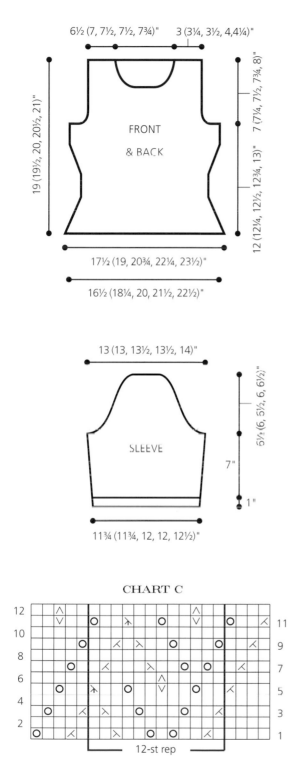

6½ (7, 7½, 7½, 7¾)"   3 (3¼, 3½, 4, 4¼)"

19 (19½, 20, 20½, 21)"

7 (7¼, 7½, 7¾, 8)"

FRONT
& BACK

12 (12¼, 12½, 12¾, 13)"

17½ (19, 20¾, 22¼, 23½)"

16½ (18¼, 20, 21½, 22½)"

13 (13, 13½, 13½, 14)"

5½ (6, 5½, 6, 6½)"

SLEEVE

7"

1"

11¾ (11¾, 12, 12, 12½)"

CHART C

12
11
10
9
8
7
6
5
4
3
2
1

12-st rep

mattatuck tee

DESIGNED BY
TABETHA HEDRICK
◼◼◼▢

A bold cable encircling
the yoke elevates
a tunic-length tee into a
cool, casual head-turner.

SIZES
XS (S, M, L, 1X, 2X, 3X)
Shown in XS.

FINISHED MEASUREMENTS
BUST 31¼ (35¼, 37¼, 40, 44, 50,
52)"/79.5 (89.5, 94.5, 101.5, 112,
127, 132)cm
LENGTH 22¾ (23¼, 24, 24½, 25,
25¾, 26½)"/57.5 (59, 61, 62, 63.5,
65.5, 67)cm

YARN & NOTIONS
4 (4, 4, 5, 5, 6, 6) hanks *Sabine*
In color #15 Mykonos

US 7 (4.5mm) circular needle,
32"/80cm long
US 5 and 6 (3.75 and 4mm)
circular needles, 24"/60cm long;
or sizes used to obtain gauge

Size 7 (4.5mm) crochet hook,
cable needle, 6 stitch markers
(4 of them removable), scrap yarn

GAUGES
20 sts and 29 rnds = 4"/10cm in
St st with largest needle.

28 sts and 25 rows = 4"/10cm in
cable pat with largest needle.
Take time to check your gauges.

GLOSSARY
2-ST RC Sl next st to cn and hold to *back*, k1, k1 from cn.
6-ST RC Sl 3 sts to cn and hold to *back*, k3, k3 from cn.
6-ST LC Sl 3 sts to cn and hold to *front*, k3, k3 from cn.

CABLE PATTERN
(over 34 sts)
ROW 1 (RS) K1, p3, 2-st RC, p2, 6-st LC, k6, 6-st RC, p2, 2-st RC, p3, k1.
ROW 2 AND ALL WS ROWS K4, p2, k2, p18, k2, p2, k4
ROW 3 K1, p3, 2-st RC, p2, k18, p2, 2-st RC, p3, k1.
ROW 5 K1, p3, 2-st RC, p2, k3, 6-st RC, 6-st LC, k3, p2, 2-st RC, p3, k1.
ROW 7 K1, p3, 2-st RC, p2, k18, p2, 2-st RC, p3, k1.
ROW 8 Rep row 2.
Rep rows 1–8 for cable pat.

PROVISIONAL CAST-ON
Using scrap yarn and crochet hook, chain the number of sts to cast on plus a few extra. Cut a tail and pull the tail through the last chain. With knitting needle and yarn, pick up and knit the stated number of stitches through the "purl bumps" on the back of the chain. To remove scrap chain, when instructed, pull out the tail from the last crochet stitch. Gently and slowly pull on the tail to unravel the crochet stitches, carefully placing each released knit stitch on a needle.

NOTES
1) The yoke is worked flat from a provisional cast-on and grafted to form a tube. Stitches are picked up along the edge of the tube for the body and the neck and worked in the round.
2) The cable pattern can be worked from the text OR the chart.

YOKE
Cast on 34 sts using provisional cast-on method. Do *not* join.
Work in cable pat following chart or text for 32 (36, 36, 40, 44, 55, 55) rows. Place marker A at beg of last row. Do *not* slip this marker every row.
Work 80 (84, 92, 100, 108, 135, 138) rows more. Place marker B at beg of last row.
Work 64 (72, 72, 80, 88, 110, 110) rows more. Place marker C at beg of last row.
Work 80 (84, 92, 100, 108, 135, 138) rows more. Place marker D at beg of last row.

mattatuck tee

Cont in pat for 31 (35, 35, 39, 43, 55, 55) rows more. Carefully remove scrap yarn from provisional cast-on, placing open sts on a needle. Graft cast-on sts to last row of sts using Kitchener st. Turn yoke so edge with markers is at top.

BODY

With RS facing and largest needle, beg at marker A, pick up and k 64 (67, 74, 80, 87, 90, 90) sts evenly along edge to marker B, remove markers A and B, cast on 14 (21, 19, 20, 23, 35, 40) sts, beg at marker C, pick up and k 64 (67, 74, 80, 87, 90, 90) sts evenly along edge to marker D, cast on 7 (10, 10, 10, 11, 17, 20) sts, place marker (pm) for beg of rnd, cast on 7 (11, 9, 10, 12, 18, 20) sts—156 (176, 186, 200, 220, 250, 260) sts.
Join to work in the rnd, k78 (88, 93, 100, 110, 125, 130), pm for side seam, k to end of rnd. K 8 rnds more.

SHAPE WAIST

NEXT (DEC) RND [Ssk, k to 2 sts before marker, k2tog, sl marker] twice—4 sts dec'd. Rep dec rnd every 0 (0, 24th, 0, 0, 0, 0) round 0 (0, 1, 0, 0, 0, 0) more times—152 (172, 178, 196, 216, 246, 256) sts.
Work even until body measures 8¼ (8¼, 8¾, 8¾, 9, 9, 9½)"/21 (21, 22, 22, 23, 25, 24)cm from pick-up edge.
NEXT (INC) RND [K1, M1, k to 1 st before marker, M1, k1, sl marker] twice—4 sts inc'd.
Rep inc rnd every 9th (39th, 13th, 13th, 13th, 10th, 13th) rnd 1 (1, 3, 3, 3, 3, 1) times more, then every 10th (0, 0, 0, 11th, 14th) rnd 3 (0, 0, 0, 0, 1, 2) times—172 (180, 194, 212, 232, 266, 272) sts. Work even until body measures 16 (16, 16½, 16½, 16¾, 17, 17¼)"/ 40.5 (40.5, 42, 42, 42.5, 43, 44)cm.
NEXT (TURNING) RND Purl.
Knit 6 rnds even. Bind off loosely.

NECKLINE

With RS facing and US 6 (4mm) needle, pick up and k 190 (210, 220, 240, 240, 260, 260) sts evenly around upper edge of cable yoke. Join to work in the rnd.
DEC RND 1 [K2tog, k1, p2] 38 (42, 44, 48, 48, 52, 52) times—152 (168, 176, 192, 192, 208, 208) sts.
NEXT RND *K2, p2; rep from * around.
Rep last rnd 6 (7, 8, 10, 11, 13, 14) times more. Change to US 5 (3.75mm) needles.

DEC RND 2 [K2, p2tog] 38 (42, 44, 48, 48, 52, 52) times—114 (126, 132, 144, 144, 156, 156) sts.
NEXT RND *K2, p1; rep from * around.
Rep last rnd 6 (8, 9, 11, 11, 13, 15) times more or until yoke measures 6¾ (7¼, 7½, 8, 8¼, 8¾, 9¼)"/17 (18.5, 19, 20.5, 21, 22, 23.5)cm from underarm. Bind off loosely in pat.

FINISHING

Block piece to measurements, being careful to let the neckline ribbing relax without stretching too much.

HEM

Fold hem along turning ridge to inside of sweater, pinning as you go around. Whip stitch edge in place. ✳

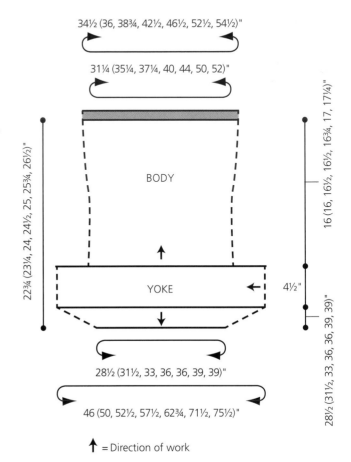

34½ (36, 38¾, 42½, 46½, 52½, 54½)"

31¼ (35¼, 37¼, 40, 44, 50, 52)"

BODY

16 (16, 16½, 16½, 16¾, 17, 17¼)"

22¾ (23¼, 24, 24½, 25, 25¾, 26½)"

YOKE

4½"

28½ (31½, 33, 36, 36, 39, 39)"

↑ = Direction of work

28½ (31½, 33, 36, 36, 39, 39)"

46 (50, 52½, 57½, 62¾, 71½, 75½)"

22

Stitch Key

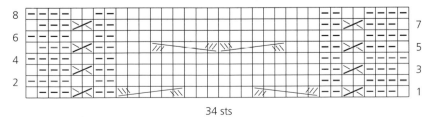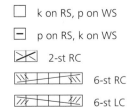

	k on RS, p on WS
−	p on RS, k on WS
⋈	2-st RC
	6-st RC
	6-st LC

34 sts

sheridan shawl

DESIGNED BY
MARIE GRACE SMITH

A pop of color in the striped border and a pretty picot edging add modern and feminine twists to a cozy garter-stitch shawl.

FINISHED MEASUREMENTS
WINGSPAN 40"/101cm
LENGTH 20"/51cm

YARN & NOTIONS
3 balls *Tenzing* in color
#02 Sage (MC)
1 ball each in colors #13 Thistle (A),
#12 Espresso (B), and
#01 Rhone Night (C)

US 6 (4mm) circular needle,
32"/80cm long, *or size used
to obtain gauge*

Stitch markers

GAUGE
24 sts and 38 rows = 4"/10cm
in garter st with US 6 (4mm) needle.
Take time to check your gauge.

GLOSSARY
CABLE CAST-ON
1) Make a slip knot on LH needle. Insert RH needle through loop and wrap yarn as if to knit.
2) Draw yarn through loop to make a st, but do not drop st from LH needle.
3) Slip new st to LH needle—2 sts on LH needle
4) *Insert RH needle between 2 sts on LH needle.
5) Wrap yarn around needle as if to knit and pull yarn through to make a new st.
6) Place new st on LH needle. Rep from *, always inserting RH needle through last 2 sts on LH needle, until desired number of sts is cast on.

sheridan shawl

NOTE
Shawl is worked back and forth in rows. Circular needle is used to accommodate large number of sts. Do not join.

SHAWL
With MC, cast on 8 sts.
ROW 1 (RS) K1, kfb, k4, kfb, k1—10 sts.
ROW 2 K1, kfb, k2, yo, place marker (pm), k2, yo, k2, kfb, k1—14 sts.
ROW 3 K1, kfb, k to last 2 sts, kfb, k1—2 sts inc'd.
ROW 4 K1, kfb, k to marker, yo, sl marker, k2, sl marker, yo, k to last 2 sts, kfb, k1—4 sts inc'd.
Rep rows 3 and 4 for 44 times more, then row 3 once—286 sts. Piece measures approx 13½"/32.5cm from beg, measured along center spine.
NEXT ROW (WS) Purl.
NEXT ROW Rep row 4—290 sts.
NEXT ROW Purl.

BEGIN STRIPE PATTERN
ROW 1 (RS) With A, K1, kfb, k to marker, yo, sl marker, k2, sl marker, yo, k to last 2 sts, kfb, k1—4 sts inc'd.
ROW 2 Purl.
ROW 3 Rep row 1.
ROW 4 Knit.
ROW 5 Rep row 1.
ROW 6 Purl.
Rep rows 1–6 in color sequence as foll: 6 rows B, 6 rows C, 6 rows A, 6 rows B—350 sts.
With C, rep rows 1–4 once, then rows 3 and 4 once more—362 sts.

PICOT BIND-OFF
With A, bind off 2 sts. *Using cable cast-on method, cast on 3 sts, bind off 7 sts; rep from * until all sts have been bound off.✶

darlington dress

DESIGNED BY
CAROLINE FRYAR

Five colors flow into one another for an ombré effect that's captivating from top to bottom.

SIZES
XS (S, M, L, XL) Shown in XS.

FINISHED MEASUREMENTS
BUST 32 (34, 36, 40, 44)"/81 (86.5, 91.5, 101.5, 111.5)cm
LENGTH 34 (34¾, 35¾, 37½, 39)"/86.5 (101, 9.5, 95, 99)cm
UPPER ARM 12 (12, 14, 14, 14)"/30.5 (30.5, 35.5, 35.5, 35.5)cm

YARN & NOTIONS
2 hanks *Herriot* in color #02 Heartwood (C1)
1 (1, 2, 2, 2) hanks *Herriot* in color #08 Sycamore (C2)
2 hanks *Herriot* in color #06 River Birch (C3)
3 (3, 3, 4, 4) hanks *Herriot* in color #09 Travertine (C4)
2 (2, 2, 3, 3) hanks *Herriot* in color #01 Talc (C5)

US 5 (3.75mm) double-pointed needles and circular needle, 24"/60cm long, *or size used to obtain gauge*

Stitch markers, stitch holders, tapestry needle

GAUGE
24 sts and 26 rnds = 4"/10cm in ombre chart pat with US 5 (3.75mm) needles.
Take time to check your gauge.

GLOSSARY
K1, P1 RIB
(over an even number of sts)
RND 1 *K1, p1; rep from * to end.
Rep rnd 1 for k1, p1 rib.

SHORT ROW WRAP & TURN (W&T)
on RS row (on WS row)
1) Wyib (wyif), sl next st purlwise.
2) Move yarn between the needles to the front (back).
3) Sl the same st back to LH needle. Turn work.
One st is wrapped.
4) When working wrapped st, insert RH needle under wrap and work it tog with corresponding st on needle to close or hide wrap.

darlington dress

SEWN BIND-OFF

1) Cut yarn, leaving a tail 3 times the circumference of the skirt hem, and thread through tapestry needle.

2) Insert needle purlwise through first 2 sts on knitting needle, and pull tight.

3) Insert tapestry needle knitwise into first st and pull tight. Drop st from knitting needle.

Rep steps 2 and 3 until all sts have been bound off.

BACK

With circular needle and C1, cast on 216 (228, 240, 264, 288) sts. Join, being careful not to twist sts, and place marker (pm) for beg of rnd.

Work 10 rnds in k1, p1 rib.

NEXT (DEC) RND [K16 (17, 18, 20, 22), k2tog] 12 times—204 (216, 228, 252, 276) sts.

Work 0 (1, 2, 3, 4) rnds even.

BEGIN OMBRÉ CHART

NEXT RND With C1 for MC and C2 for CC, work 12-st rep of ombré chart 17 (18, 19, 21, 23) times around. Cont to work chart in this way until rnd 35 is complete. Break C1.

NEXT (DEC) RND With C2, [k15 (16, 17, 19, 21), k2tog] 12 times—192 (204, 216, 240, 264) sts.

Work 0 (1, 2, 3, 4) rnds even.

NEXT RND With C2 for MC and C3 for CC, work 12-st chart rep 16 (17, 18, 20, 22) times around. Cont to work in this way until rnd 35 is complete. Break C2.

With C3, work 0 (1, 2, 3, 4) rnds even.

NEXT (DEC) RND [K14 (15, 16, 18, 20), k2tog] 12 times—180 (192, 204, 228, 252) sts.

NEXT RND With C3 for MC and C4 for CC, work 12-st chart rep 15 (16, 17, 19, 21) times around. Cont to work in this way until rnd 35 is complete. Piece measures approx 18¼ (18¾, 19, 19½, 20)"/46.5 (47.5, 48, 49.5, 51)cm from beg. Break C3.

NEXT (DEC) RND With C4, [k13 (14, 15, 17, 19), k2tog] 12 times—168 (180, 192, 216, 240) sts.

Work 0 (1, 2, 3, 4) rnds even.

With C4 for MC and C5 for CC, rep rnds 1–11 of ombré chart.

NEXT (INC) RND With C4, [k14 (15, 16, 18, 20), M1] 12 times—180 (192, 204, 228, 252) sts.

NEXT RND With C4 for MC and C5 for CC, work 12-st rep of chart rnd 13 for 15 (16, 17, 19, 21) times around. Cont to work chart in this way until rnd 35 is complete. Break C4.

NEXT (INC) RND With C5, [k15 (16, 17, 19, 21), M1] 12 times—192 (204, 216, 240, 264) sts.

Body measures approx 24 (25, 25½, 26½, 27)"/61 (63.5, 64.5, 67, 68.5)cm from beg. Set body aside.

SLEEVES

With C4 and dpns, cast on 60 (60, 72, 72, 72) sts. Join, being careful not to twist sts, and pm for beg of rnd.

Work 10 rnds in k1, p1 rib.

BEG OMBRÉ CHART

NEXT 4 RNDS With C4 for MC and C5 for CC, work 12-st chart rep 5 (5, 6, 6, 6) times around.

NEXT (INC) RND M1, cont in chart pat as established to last st, M1, k1—2 sts inc'd.

Cont in pat as established and rep inc rnd every 5th rnd 5 times more, working new sts into chart pat—72 (72, 84, 84, 84) sts.

Work even until rnd 34 is complete.

NEXT RND Work rnd 35 of ombré chart as established to last 3 (3, 6, 6, 6) sts. Sleeve measures approx 7"/18cm. Make 2nd sleeve.

YOKE

NEXT (JOINING) RND With C5, beg at beg-of-rnd marker on body (right underarm), k 3 (3, 6, 6, 6) sts and place them on st holder, pm, k 90 (96, 96, 108, 120) back sts, place next 6 (6, 12, 12, 12) sts on st holder, place 6 (6, 12, 12, 12) sts from left sleeve on st holder, pm, k 66 (66, 72, 72, 72) sts of left sleeve, pm, k 93 (99, 102, 114, 126) front sts and place last 3 (3, 6, 6, 6) sts worked on st holder, place 6 (6, 12, 12, 12) sts from 2nd sleeve on holder, pm and k 66 (66, 72, 72, 72) sleeve sts. Pm for beg of rnd—312 (324, 336, 360, 384) sts.

BEG OMBRÉ CHART

RND 1 With C5 for MC and C4 for CC, work 12-st chart rep 26 (27, 28, 30, 32) times around. Cont in this way until rnd 23 (23, 25, 27, 29) of ombré chart is complete.

NEXT (DEC) RND With C4, *k1, k2tog; rep from * around—208 (216, 224, 240, 256) sts.

darlington dress

BEG YOKE CHART
Beg with rnd 17 (19, 21, 23, 25), work 4-st rep 52 (54, 56, 60, 64) times around.
Cont to work in this way until rnd 29 is complete.

For sizes S (M, L, XL) only:
Work 1 rnd in C4, then work rnds 1 through 2 (4, 6, 8) of yoke chart, with C4 for MC and C3 for CC.

For all sizes:
With C4, *k2, k2tog; rep from * around—156 (162, 168, 180, 192) sts. Break C3 and cont with C4.

SHAPE NECK
Work short rows to shape back neck as foll:
ROW 1 (RS) K45 (48, 48, 54, 60), w&t.
ROW 2 (WS) P41 (44, 44, 50, 56), w&t.
ROW 3 (RS) K37 (40, 40, 46, 52), w&t.
ROW 4 (WS) P33 (36, 36, 42, 48), w&t.
ROW 5 (RS) K29 (32, 32, 38, 44), w&t.
ROW 6 (WS) P25 (28, 28, 34, 40), w&t.
ROW 7 (RS) K21 (24, 24, 30, 36), w&t.
ROW 8 (WS) P17 (20, 20, 26, 32), w&t.

For sizes L (XL) only:
ROW 9 (RS) K22 (28), w&t.
ROW 10 (WS) P18 (24), w&t.

For all sizes:
With C4, k 1 rnd, closing wraps as you come to them.
With C4 for MC and C3 for CC, cont to work yoke chart as established until rnd 5 (10, 14, 18, 25) is complete.
NEXT (DEC) RND *K1, k2tog; rep from * around—104 (108, 112, 120, 128) sts rem.
With C3, work 10 rnds in k1, p1 rib.
Bind off neck sts using sewn bind-off or another stretchy bind-off.

FINISHING
Graft together underarm sts using Kitchener stitch.
Weave in ends and block to measurements. ✳

17¼ (18, 18½, 20, 21¼)"

34 (34¾, 35¾, 37½, 39)"

7"

BODY

10 (10, 12, 12, 12)"

12 (12, 14, 14, 14)"

13 (10¼, 10¾, 11½, 12½)"

5¾ (5¾, 6, 6½, 6½)"

6¾ (17½, 17½, 18, 18½)"

1½"

34 (36, 38, 42, 46)"

27½ (30, 32, 36, 40)"

32 (34, 36, 40, 44)"

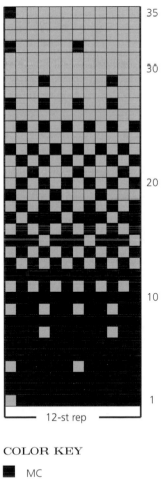

OMBRE CHART

35

30

20

10

1

12-st rep

YOKE CHART

29

20

10

1

4-st rep

COLOR KEY

■ MC

■ CC

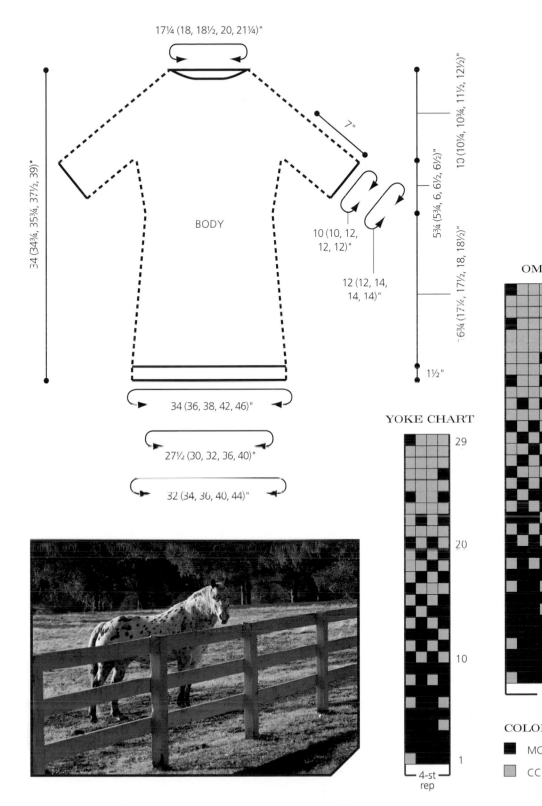

31

silverton top and cowl

DESIGNED BY
MELISSA LEAPMAN

■■■▢

Looking for versatility?
Knit up a lacy vest with
a removable ribbed cowl
and wear it with ease
throughout the seasons.

SIZES
XS (S, M, L, 1X)
Shown in XS.

FINISHED MEASUREMENTS
BUST 33½ (37, 41½, 45, 49½)"/85
(94, 105.5, 114.5, 125.5)cm
LENGTH 21½ (22, 23, 23½,
24½)"/54.5 (56, 58.5, 59.5, 62)cm

YARN & NOTIONS
5 (6, 7, 8, 9) hanks *Moonshine*
in color #01 Dew

US 6 and 7 (4 and 4.5mm)
straight needles

US 6 (4mm) circular needle,
16"/40cm long, *or sizes used
to obtain gauge*

Cable needle, two stitch markers

GAUGE
20 sts = 4"/10cm and
32 rows = 5"/12.5cm in chart
pat with larger needles.
Take time to check your gauge.

NOTE
When working sleeve shaping into chart pat, always work a
paired dec with a yo, or work sts in rev St st until there are
sufficient sts to work in pat. If a row begins or ends with
a yo, then omit the yo and its corresponding dec and work
these sts into rev St st.

GLOSSARY
K2, P2 RIB
(multiple of 4 sts plus 2)
ROW 1 (RS) K2, *p2, k2; rep from * to end.
ROW 2 P2, *k2, p2; rep from * to end.
Rep rows 1 and 2 for k2, p2 rib.

2-ST RC Sl 1 st to cn and hold to *back*, k1tbl, k1tbl from cn.
2-ST LC Sl 1 st to cn and hold to *front*, k1tbl, k1tbl from cn.
2-ST RPC Sl 1 st to cn and hold to *back*, k1tbl, p1 from cn.
2-ST LPC Sl 1 st to cn and hold to *front*, p1, k1tbl from cn.

BACK
With smaller needles, cast on 82 (90, 102, 110, 122) sts.
Work in k2, p2 rib for 6 rows, inc 1 st each side of last row
and end with a WS row—84 (92, 104, 112, 124) sts. Change
to larger needles.

BEG CHART PAT
ROW 1 (RS) P3 (7, 3, 7, 3), place marker (pm), work first 9 sts of
chart to rep line, work 20-st rep 3 (3, 4, 4, 5) times, work last 9
sts of chart, pm, p3 (7, 3, 7, 3). Keeping 3 (7, 3, 7, 3) sts each
side in rev St st (p on RS and k on WS), cont to work in this way
through chart row 32, then rep rows 1–32 for lace pat. Work
even until piece measures 12¼ (12¼, 12¾, 12¾, 13¼)"/31
(31, 32.5, 32.5, 33.5)cm from beg, end with a WS row.

SHAPE SLEEVES
Inc 1 st each side on next row, then every row 10 times more—
106 (114, 126, 134, 146) sts. Mark beg and end of last row
for beg of armholes. Work even until armhole measures 7½ (8,
8½, 9, 9½)"/19 (20.5, 21.5, 23, 24)cm above marked row, end
with a WS row. Bind off all sts.

FRONT
Work same as back until armhole measures 4½ (5, 5½, 6,
6½)"/11.5 (12.5, 14, 15, 16.5)cm above marked row,
end with a WS row.

silverton top and cowl

SHAPE NECK
NEXT ROW (RS) Work across first 46 (50, 55, 59, 64) sts, join a 2nd ball of yarn and bind off center 14 (14, 16, 16, 18) sts, work to end. Working both sides at once, bind off from each neck edge 5 sts once, then 2 sts once. Dec 1 st from each neck edge on next row, then every row 3 times more—35 (39, 44, 48, 53) sts each side. Work even until piece measures same length as back to shoulder, end with a WS row. Bind off each side.

FINISHING
Block pieces to measurements. Sew shoulder and side/sleeve seams.

NECKBAND
With RS facing and circular needle, pick up and k 19 sts evenly spaced along left neck edge, 14 (14, 16, 16, 18) sts along front neck, 19 sts evenly spaced along right neck edge, then 36 (36, 38, 38, 40) sts along back neck edge—88 (88, 92, 92, 96) sts. Join and pm for beg of rnds. Work around in k2, p2 rib for 5 rnds. Bind off loosely in rib.

SLEEVE BANDS
With RS facing and circular needle, pick up and k 76 (80, 84, 92, 96) sts evenly spaced around armhole edge. Join and pm for beg of rnds. Work around in k2, p2 rib for 5 rnds. Bind off loosely in rib.

DETACHED COWL
With smaller needles, cast on 56 sts. Work in k2, p2 rib for 22 (23, 24, 25, 26)"/56 (58.5, 61, 63.5, 66)cm, end with a WS row. Bind off in rib. Sew cast-on edge to bind-off edge.✷

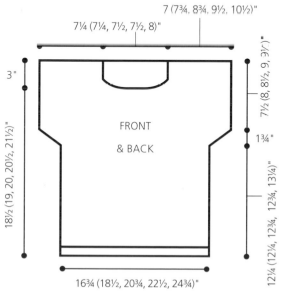

7 (7¾, 8¾, 9½, 10½)"

7¼ (7¼, 7½, 7½, 8)"

3"

7½ (8, 8½, 9, 9½)"

1¾"

18½ (19, 20, 20½, 21½)"

FRONT
& BACK

12¼ (12¼, 12¾, 12¾, 13¼)"

16¾ (18½, 20¾, 22½, 24¾)"

silverton top and cowl

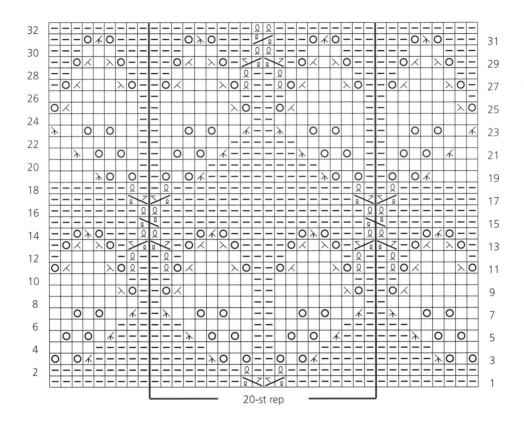

20-st rep

STITCH KEY

☐	k on RS, p on WS	⊙	yo
⊟	p on RS, k on WS	Ⴍ	k1 tbl on RS, p1 tbl on WS
⟋	k2tog	⟋Ⴍ	2-st RC
⟍	SKP	Ⴍ⟍	2-st LC
⟀	sssk	⟋Ⴍ	2-st RPC
⟋	k3tog	Ⴍ⟍	2-st LPC

36

cody hat and cowl

DESIGNED BY
ALISON GREEN
◼️◼️◻️◻️

Play with palettes in an accessory set that catches the eye with its unique combination of two-color cables and dotted columns.

SIZES
S/M (L)
Shown in S/M.

FINISHED MEASUREMENTS
HAT BRIM 17½ (19¾)"/44.5 (50)cm
COWL CIRCUMFERENCE 21"/53.5cm
COWL LENGTH 8"/20.5cm

YARN & NOTIONS
2 hanks *Herriot* each in colors #1000 Oatmeal (A) and #1002 Pansy (B)

US 4 and 6 (3.5 and 4mm) circular needle, 16"/40cm long

US 6 (4 mm) double-pointed needles (for hat only) *or sizes used to obtain gauge*

Stitch marker, cable needle

GAUGE
33½ sts and 26 rnds = 4"/10cm in chart 1 pat with larger needle.
Take time to check your gauge.

GLOSSARY
4-ST RC Sl 2 sts to cn and hold to *back*, k2, k2 from cn.
4-ST LC Sl 2 sts to cn and hold to *front*, k2, k2 from cn.
8-ST RC Sl 4 sts to cn and hold to *back*, k4, k4 from cn.
8-ST LC Sl 4 sts to cn and hold to *front*, k4, k4 from cn.

GARTER STITCH
(over any number of sts)
RND 1 Purl.
RND 2 Knit.
Rep rnds 1 and 2 for garter st.

HAT
With smaller needle and A, cast on 88 (99) sts. Place marker (pm) for beg of rnd and join, being careful not to twist sts. Work in garter st for 7 rnds.
NEXT (INC) RND Kfb in each st around—176 (198) sts.
Change to larger needle.

BEGIN CHART 1
RND 1 Work the 22-st rep of chart 1 for 8 (9) times around. Cont to work in this way until rnd 8 is complete. Rep rows 1–8 three times more.

BEG CHART 2
NOTE Change to dpns when sts no longer fit comfortably on circular needle.
ROW 1 Work st-rep 8 (9) times around—144 (162) sts.
Cont to work in this way until rnd 16 is complete.
NEXT (DEC) RND With A, k2tog around—8 (9) sts.
Cut yarn and thread both strands through rem sts. Pull taut and secure.

cody hat and cowl

COWL

With smaller circular needle and B, cast on 124 sts. Pm for beg of rnd and join, being careful not to twist sts. Work in garter st for 7 rnds.

NEXT INC RND *Kfb, [k1, kfb] twice; rep from * around—198 sts. Change to larger needle.

BEGIN CHART 1

RND 1 Work the 22-st rep of chart 1 for 8 (9) times around. Cont to work in this way until rnd 8 is complete. Rep rows 1–8 four times more.

Cut A. Change to smaller needle and with B, knit 1 rnd.

NEXT (DEC) RND With B, *k2tog, [k1, k2tog] twice; rep from * around—124 sts.

Beg with rnd 2, work in garter st for 7 rnds. Bind off.

FINISHING

Wash and gently block.✳

Choose tonal hues for a more subtle look. .

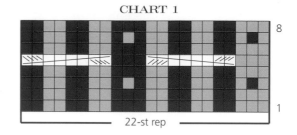

CHART 1

8

1

22-st rep

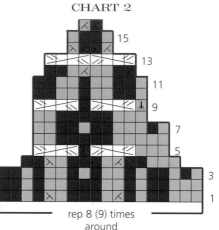

CHART 2

15

13

11

9

7

5

3

1

rep 8 (9) times around

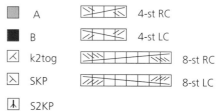

COLOR & STITCH KEY

▨	A		▨	4-st RC
■	B		▨	4-st LC
◹	k2tog		▨	8-st RC
◺	SKP		▨	8-st LC
⟰	S2KP			

40

carroll cardigan

**DESIGNED BY
MARIE GRACE SMITH**

◼◼◼◻

The pretty features of a
raglan cardigan include a
boat neck, waist shaping,
and a leafy lace pattern
on the sleeves.

SIZES
XS (S, M, L, 1X, 2X)
Shown in XS.

FINISHED MEASUREMENTS
BUST (CLOSED) 31¼ (35¼, 39¼,
43¼, 47¼, 51¼)"/79 (90, 99.5, 110,
120, 130.5)cm
LENGTH 24 (24½, 24¾, 25¼, 25¼,
26)"/61 (62, 63, 64, 64, 66)cm
UPPER ARM 12½ (13, 14, 14½, 16,
18)"/31.5 (33, 35.5, 37, 40.5, 45.5)cm

YARN & NOTIONS
4 (5, 5, 6, 6, 7) hanks *Sabine* in color
#17 Poppy

US 7 (4.5mm) straight needles
US 5 (3.75mm) circular needle,
16"/32cm long, and straight needles
or sizes used to obtain gauge

Stitch holders, six ½"/12mm buttons

GAUGES
19 sts and 30 rows = 4"/10cm
in St st with larger needles.

20 sts and 26 rows = 4"/10cm
in chart pat (washed and blocked)
with larger needles.
Take time to check your gauges.

GLOSSARY
M1R Insert LH needle from back to front under the strand
between last st worked and next st on LH needle. K into
the front loop to twist the st.
M1L Insert LH needle from front to back under the strand
between last st worked and next st on LH needle. K into
the back loop to twist the st.

BACK
With smaller needle, cast on 76 (86, 95, 105, 114, 124) sts.
NEXT ROW (RS) Knit.
NEXT ROW Purl.
Rep last 2 rows once more.
Change to larger needles.
Cont in St st for 10 rows more.

SHAPE WAIST
NEXT (DEC) ROW (RS) K5, ssk, k to last 7 sts, k2tog, k5.
Cont in St st and rep dec row every 12th row twice more—
70 (80, 89, 99, 108, 118) sts.
Work even until piece measures 7½"/19cm from beg.
NEXT (INC) ROW (RS) K5, M1R, k to last 5 sts, M1L, k5.
Rep inc row every 12th row twice more—76 (86, 95, 105,
114, 124) sts.
Work even until piece measures 15¾ (15¾, 15¾, 15, 14¾,
14)"/40 (40, 40, 38, 37.5, 35.5)cm from beg, end with a
WS row.

SHAPE RAGLAN
Bind off 7 (7, 8, 9, 10, 10) sts at beg of next 2 rows.
NEXT (DEC) ROW (RS) K1, ssk, k to last 3 sts, k2tog, k1.
Rep dec row every 6th row 4 (0, 0, 0, 0, 0) times more,
then every 4th row 4 (10, 8, 9, 9, 10) times, then every 2nd
row 0 (3, 8, 10, 11, 15) times.
Place rem 44 (44, 45, 47, 52, 52) sts on a st holder for back
neck.

LEFT FRONT
With smaller needle, cast on 38 (43, 48, 53, 57, 62) sts.
NEXT ROW (RS) Knit.
NEXT ROW Purl.
Rep last 2 rows once more.
Change to larger needles.
Cont in St st for 10 rows more.

carroll cardigan

SHAPE WAIST

NEXT (DEC) ROW (RS) K5, ssk, k across.
Cont in St st and rep dec row every 12th row twice more—35 (40, 45, 50, 54, 59) sts.
Work even until piece measures 7½"/19cm from beg.
NEXT (INC) ROW (RS) K5, M1R, k to end.
Rep inc row every 12th row twice more—38 (43, 48, 53, 57, 62) sts.
Work even until piece measures same as back to armhole, end with a WS row.

SHAPE RAGLAN

NEXT ROW (WS) Bind off 7 (7, 8, 9, 10, 10) sts, p to end.
NEXT (DEC) ROW (RS) K1, ssk, k to end—1 st dec'd.
Rep dec row every 6th row 4 (0, 0, 0, 0, 0) times more, then every 4th row 4 (10, 8, 9, 9, 10) times, then every 2nd row 0 (3, 8, 10, 11, 15) times.
Place rem 22 (22, 23, 24, 26, 26) sts on a st holder.

RIGHT FRONT

With smaller needle, cast on 38 (43, 48, 53, 57, 62) sts.
NEXT ROW (RS) Knit.
NEXT ROW Purl.
Rep last 2 rows once more.
Change to larger needles.
Cont in St st for 10 more rows.

SHAPE WAIST

NEXT (DEC) ROW (RS) K to last 7 sts, k2tog, k5.
Cont in St st and rep dec row every 12th row twice more—35 (40, 45, 50, 54, 59) sts.
Work even until piece measures 7½"/19cm from beg.
NEXT (INC) ROW (RS) K to last 5 sts, M1L, k5.
Rep inc row every 12th row twice more—38 (43, 48, 53, 57, 62) sts.
Work even until piece measures same as back to armhole, end with a RS row.

SHAPE RAGLAN

NEXT ROW (WS) Bind off 7 (7, 8, 9, 10, 10), work across.
NEXT (DEC) ROW (RS) K to last 3 sts, k2tog, k1—1 st dec'd.
Rep dec row every 6th row 4 (0, 0, 0, 0, 0) times more, then every 4th row 4 (10, 8, 9, 9, 10) times, then every 2nd row 0 (3, 8, 10, 11, 15) times.
Place rem 22 (22, 23, 24, 26, 26) sts on a st holder.

SLEEVE

With smaller needles, cast on 43 (51, 51, 51, 59, 67) sts.
NEXT ROW (RS) Knit.
NEXT ROW Purl.
Rep last 2 rows once more.
Change to larger needles.

BEGIN CHART

NEXT ROW (RS) Work row 1 of chart to rep line, work 8-st rep 4 (5, 5, 5, 6, 7) times across, work to end of chart.
Cont to work in this way until row 16 of chart is complete, rep rows 1–16 of chart until piece measures 4"/10cm from beg, end with a WS row.

SHAPE SLEEVE

Cont in chart pat as established, working inc'd sts into pat.
NEXT (INC) ROW (RS) K1, M1R, work in pat to last st, M1L, k1—2 sts inc'd.
Rep inc row 10 (14, 12, 10, 10, 8) rows 9 (6, 8, 10, 10, 11) times more—63 (65, 69, 73, 81, 91) sts.
Work even until piece measures 20½ (21, 21, 21½, 21½, 22)"/52 (53.5, 53.5, 54.5, 54.5, 56)cm from beg, end with a WS row.

SHAPE RAGLAN

Bind off 7 (7, 8, 9, 10, 10) sts at beg of next 2 rows.
DEC ROW (RS) K1, ssk, work to last 3 sts, k2tog, k1.
Rep dec row every 4th row 4 (5, 5, 8, 6, 5) times more, then every 2nd row 9 (9, 10, 8, 13, 19) times.
Place rem 21 sts on a st holder.

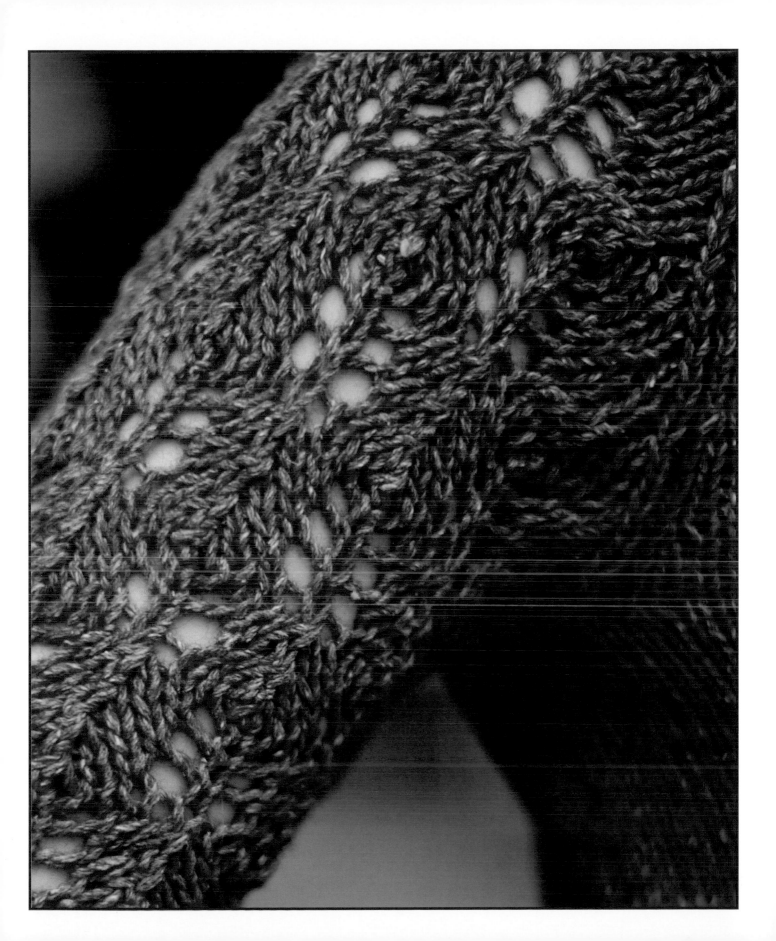

carroll cardigan

FINISHING
Gently block pieces to measurements. Sew raglan seams.

NECKBAND
Place all sts from st holders on circular needle.
NEXT ROW (RS) Purl.
NEXT ROW Knit.
Rep last 2 rows once more.
Bind off loosely.

LEFT FRONT BAND
Beg at upper edge with RS facing, pick up and k 106
(110, 112, 112, 114, 114) sts.
NEXT ROW Knit.
Bind off.

RIGHT FRONT BAND
Beg at lower edge with RS facing, pick up and k 106
(110, 112, 112, 114, 114) sts.
NEXT (BUTTONHOLE) ROW K4, [k2tog, yo, k14 (14, 15,
15, 15, 15)] 6 times, k6 (10, 6, 6, 8, 8).
Bind off.✳

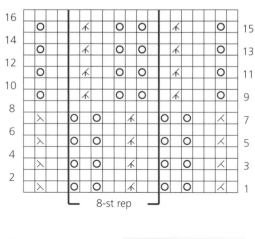

8-st rep

STITCH KEY

☐	k on RS, p on WS
⊠	k2tog
⊠	SKP
◯	yo
⊼	k3tog

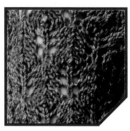

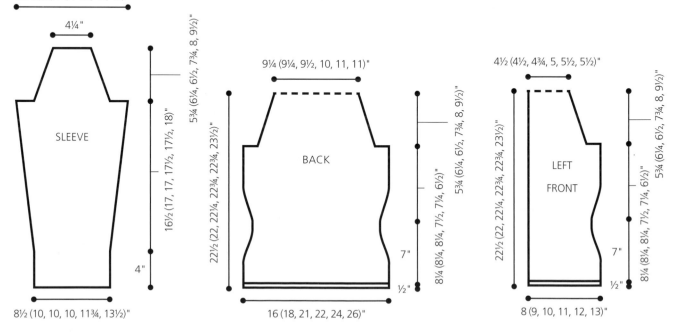

SLEEVE

12½ (13, 14, 14½, 16, 18)"

4¼"

5¾ (6¼, 6½, 7¾, 8, 9½)"

16½ (17, 17, 17½, 17½, 18)"

4"

8½ (10, 10, 10, 11¾, 13½)"

BACK

9¼ (9¼, 9½, 10, 11, 11)"

5¾ (6¼, 6½, 7¾, 8, 9½)"

22½ (22, 22¼, 22¾, 22¾, 23½)"

8¼ (8¼, 8¼, 7½, 7¼, 6½)"

7"

½"

16 (18, 21, 22, 24, 26)"

LEFT FRONT

4½ (4½, 4¾, 5, 5½, 5½)"

5¾ (6¼, 6½, 7¾, 8, 9½)"

22½ (22, 22¼, 22¾, 22¾, 23½)"

8¼ (8¼, 8¼, 7½, 7¼, 6½)"

7"

½"

8 (9, 10, 11, 12, 13)"

fayette stole

DESIGNED BY
ADRIENNE KU
■■■□

You'll feel tickled pink wrapped in this super-soft stole that features a geometric lace pattern knit in a bold berry hue.

FINISHED MEASUREMENTS
Approximately 16 x 48"/40.5 x 122cm

YARN & NOTIONS
1 ball *Findley* in color #26 Mulberry

US 5 (3.75mm) straight needles *or size used to obtain gauge*

Size F/5 (3.77mm) crochet hook, stitch markers (optional)

GAUGE
20 sts and 28 rows = 4"/10cm in lace pat after blocking with US 5 (3.75mm) needles.
Take time to check your gauge.

GLOSSARY
CROCHET CAST-ON
1) Make a slip knot and place on the crochet hook.
2) Hold the hook in front of the knitting needle with the working yarn behind the needle.
3) With the crochet hook, draw a loop through the slip knot. The yarn around the knitting needle forms the first cast-on stitch. Keeping the new loop on the crochet hook, move the working yarn to the back of the needle. Continue to form stitches in this manner, drawing each loop through the new loop on the crochet hook, until there is 1 less st on the needle than the desired number of cast-on sts.
4) Place the loop from the crochet hook on the needle to form the last cast-on stitch.

NOTE
Place markers between each 12-st pat rep, and slip markers on every row.

STOLE
Cast on 93 sts using crochet cast-on method.
SET-UP ROW (WS) Sl 1 purlwise wyif, k1, purl to last 3 sts, k1, p1, k1tbl.

BEGIN CHART
ROW 1 (RS) Work to rep line, work 12-st rep 6 times across, work to end of chart.
Cont to work in this manner until row 24 is complete. Rep rows 1–24 nineteen times more, rep row 1–14 once. Bind off as foll:
K2, *insert LH needle into fronts of sts just worked and k2tog tbl, k1; rep from * until all sts are bound off.

FINISHING
Block to open lace. ✳

fayette stole

Stitch Key

☐ k on RS, p on WS

– p on RS, k on WS

╱ k2tog

╲ SKP

O yo

Ⴢ k1 tbl

⅄ SK2P

⅄ slip 1 wyif

traverse city tunic

DESIGNED BY
TABETHA HEDRICK

The universally flattering shape of an A-line tunic is complemented by a gorgeous lace panel at the front and neckline.

SIZES
XS (S, M, L, XL)
Shown in S.

FINISHED MEASUREMENTS
BUST 35 (36, 38, 40, 42½)"/89 (91.5, 96.5, 101.5, 108)cm
LENGTH 28 (28, 28½, 29, 29½)"/71 (71, 72.5, 73.5, 75)cm
UPPER ARM 11½ (11½, 12½, 13¼, 14)"/29 (29, 32, 33.5, 35.5)cm

YARN & NOTIONS
6 (6, 7, 7, 8) balls *Findley DK* in color #11 Trylan

US 7 (4.5mm) circular needle, 16"/40cm long, and straight needles *or size used to obtain gauge*

Stitch markers

GAUGE
20 sts and 28 rows = 4"/10cm in St st with size 7 (4.5mm) needles. *Take time to check your gauge.*

NOTE
A garter (k1) selvage st is worked at the beginning and end of every row for a selvage st, and the selvage st is not calculated in the finished measurements.

BACK
Cast on 100 (104, 108, 114, 120) sts. Knit 2 rows. Then, beg with a k row, work in St st for 6 rows.

SHAPE WAIST
DEC ROW 1 (RS) K1, ssk, k to last 3 sts, k2tog, k1.
Rep dec row every 22nd row 5 times more—88 (92, 96, 102, 108) sts. Work even until piece measures 20"/51cm from beg.

SHAPE ARMHOLE
Bind off 4 (4, 4, 5, 5) sts at beg of next 2 rows.
DEC ROW (RS) K1, ssk, k to last 3 sts, k2tog, k1.
Rep dec row every other row 1 (2, 3, 4, 5) times more—76 (78, 80, 82, 86) sts. Work even until armhole measures 7¼ (7¼, 7¾, 8¼, 8¾)"/18.5 (18.5, 19.5, 21, 22)cm.

traverse city tunic

SHAPE SHOULDER
Bind off 6 (6, 7, 7, 8) sts at beg of next 4 rows, then 7 (8, 7, 8, 8) sts at beg of next 2 rows. Bind off rem 40 sts.

FRONT
Cast on 98 (102, 106, 112, 118) sts.

BEGIN LACE CHART
ROW 1 (RS) K41 (43, 45, 48, 51), place marker (pm), work row 1 of lace pat over 16 sts, pm, k41 (43, 45, 48, 51).
ROW 2 K to marker, sl marker, work row 2 of lace pat over 16 sts, sl marker, k to end.
Then cont in St st on sts each side of markers, with the 16 sts between the markers in chart pat, for 6 rows more.
DEC ROW (RS) K1, ssk, work in pats as established to last 3 sts, k2tog, k1.
Cont in pats as established, rep dec row every 22nd row 5 times more—86 (90, 94, 100, 106) sts.
Work even until piece measures 19¾"/50cm from beg (or 2 rows before beg the armhole), end with a chart row 2. At this point, sts will be added each side in the lace pat while at same time working a compensation of 1 less st in St st.
NEXT ROW (RS) Work to 1 st before marker, p2, yo, p3, p3tog, p3, [yo, p1] twice, p2, p2tog, p1, k to end.
NEXT ROW Work to 1 st before marker, k1, k2tog, k3, [yo, k1] twice, k2, k3tog, k3, yo, k2, p to last st, k1.

SHAPE ARMHOLE AND SET UP NECK
Shape armhole as for back and, AT THE SAME TIME, work lace pat expansion as foll:
ROW 1 (RS) Work to 2 sts before marker, p2, p2tog, p3, [yo, p1] twice, p2, p3tog, p3, yo, p3, work to end.
ROW 2 Work to 2 sts before marker, k3, yo, k3, k3tog, k3, [yo, k1] twice, k2, k2tog, k2, work to end.
ROW 3 Work to 3 sts before marker, p3, p2tog, p3, [yo, p1] twice, p2, p3tog, p3, yo, p4, work to last 3 sts, k2tog, k1.
ROW 4 Work to 3 sts before marker, k4, yo, k3, k3tog, k3, [yo, k1] twice, k2, k2tog, k3, work to end.
ROW 5 Work to 4 sts before marker, p2tog, p2, [yo, p1] twice, p2, p3tog, p3, [yo, p1] twice, p2, p2tog, p4, work to last 3 sts, k2tog, k1.
ROW 6 Work to 4 sts before marker, k4, k2tog, k3, [yo, k1] twice, k2, k3tog, k3, [yo, k1] twice, k1, k2tog, work to end.
ROW 7 Work to 5 sts before marker, p2tog, p2, *[p1, yo] twice, p3, p3tog, p2; rep from * once more, p1, yo, p1, work to last 3 sts, k2tog, k1.
ROW 8 Work to 5 sts before marker, k1, yo, *k3, k3tog, k2, [k1, yo] twice; rep from * once more, k3, k2tog, work to end.
Working 1 less st in St st each side of lace pat, cont lace expansion as foll:
ROW 9 Work to 1 st before lace pat (this will not be stated in foll rows), p2, yo, *p3, p3tog, p2, [p1, yo] twice; rep from * once more, p3, p2tog, p1, work in pat to end of row (this will not be stated in foll rows).
ROW 10 K1, k2tog, k2, *[k1, yo] twice, k3, k3tog, k2; rep from * once more, k1, yo, k2.
ROW 11 P3, yo, *p3, p3tog, p2, [p1, yo] twice; rep from * once more, p3, p2tog, p2.
ROW 12 K2, k2tog, k2, *[k1, yo] twice, k3, k3tog, k2; rep from * once more, k1, yo, k3.
ROW 13 P3, p2tog, p2, *[p1, yo] twice, p3, p3tog, p2; rep from * once more, p1, yo, p4.
ROW 14 K4, yo, k3, k3tog, k2, [k1, yo] twice, k3, k3tog, k2, [k1, yo] twice, k3, k2tog, k3.

SHAPE NECK
Working both sides at once with separate balls of yarn, cont lace expansion, working 1 less st in St st on each side and shape neck as foll:
(**NOTE** There will always be 16 sts in lace pat on each side of neck opening.)
ROW 1 P4, p2tog, p3, [yo, p1] twice, p2, p2tog, k2tog, join a 2nd ball of yarn to work each side of the neck separately, ssk, p1, yo, p3, p3tog, p3, yo, p5.
ROW 2 K5, yo, k3, k3tog, k3, yo, k1, p1; with 2nd ball of yarn, p1, k2tog, k3, [yo, k1] twice, k2, k2tog, k4.
ROW 3 P2tog, p3, [yo, p1] twice, p2, p3tog, p3, yo, k2tog; with 2nd ball of yarn, ssk, p5, yo, p3, p3tog, p3, yo, p1.
ROW 4 K1, yo, k3, k3tog, k3, yo, k5, p1; with 2nd ball of yarn, p1, yo, k3, k3tog, k3, [yo, k1] twice, k2, k2tog.
ROW 5 P1, p2tog, p3, [yo, p1] twice, p2, p2tog, p3, k2tog; with 2nd ball of yarn, ssk, p4, yo, p3, p3tog, p3, yo, p2.
ROW 6 K2, yo, k3, k3tog, k3, yo, k4, p1; with 2nd ball of yarn, p1, k3, k2tog, k3, [yo, k1] twice, k2, k2tog, k1.
ROW 7 P3, yo, p3, p3tog, p3, yo, p3, k2tog; with 2nd ball of yarn, ssk, p2, p2tog, p3, [yo, p1] twice, p2, p2tog, p2.
ROW 8 K2, k2tog, k3, [yo, k1] twice, k2, k2tog, k2, p1; with 2nd ball of yarn, p1, k3, yo, k3, k3tog, k3, yo, k3.

traverse city tunic

ROW 9 P4, yo, p3, p3tog, p3, yo, p2, k2tog; with 2nd ball of yarn, ssk, p1, p2tog, p3, [yo, p1] twice, p2, p2tog, p3.

ROW 10 K3, k2tog, k3, [yo, k1] twice, k2, k2tog, k1, p1; with 2nd ball of yarn, p1, k2, yo, k3, k3tog, k3, yo, k4.

ROW 11 Yo, p3, p3tog, p3, [yo, p1] twice, p2, p2tog, k2tog; with 2nd ball of yarn, ssk, p1, yo, p3, p3tog, p3, yo, p5.

ROW 12 K5, yo, k3, k3tog, k3, yo, k1, p1; with 2nd ball of yarn, p1, k2tog, k3, [yo, k1] twice, k2, k3tog, k3, yo.

ROW 13 P1, yo, p3, p3tog, p3, [yo, p1] twice, p2, k2tog; with 2nd ball of yarn, ssk, yo, p3, p3tog, p3, [yo, p1] twice, p2, p2tog.

ROW 14 K2tog, k3, [yo, k1] twice, k2, k3tog, k3, yo, p1; with 2nd ball of yarn, p1, k3, [yo, k1] twice, k2, k3tog, k3, yo, k1.

ROW 15 P1, p2tog, p3, [yo, p1] twice, p2, p2tog, p3, k2tog; with 2nd ball of yarn, ssk, p4, yo, p3, p3tog, p3, yo, p2.

ROW 16 K2, yo, k3, k3tog, k3, yo, k4, p1; with 2nd ball of yarn, p1, k3, k2tog, k3, [yo, k1] twice, k2, k2tog, k1.

ROW 17 P2, p2tog, p3, [yo, p1] twice, p2, p2tog, p2, k2tog; with 2nd ball of yarn, ssk, p3, yo, p3, p3tog, p3, yo, p3.

ROW 18 K3, yo, k3, k3tog, k3, yo, k3, p1; with 2nd ball of yarn, p1, k2, k2tog, k3, [yo, k1] twice, k2, k2tog, k2.

ROW 19 P4, yo, p3, p3tog, p3, yo, p2, k2tog; with 2nd ball of yarn, ssk, p1, p2tog, p3, [yo, p1] twice, p2, p2tog, p3.

ROW 20 K3, k2tog, k3, [yo, k1] twice, k2, k2tog, k1, p1; with 2nd ball of yarn, p1, k2, yo, k3, k3tog, k3, yo, k4.

ROW 21 P5, yo, p3, p3tog, p3, yo, p1, k2tog; with 2nd ball of yarn, ssk, p6, yo, p3, p3tog, p3, yo, k11.

ROW 22 Yo, k3, k3tog, k3, yo, k6, p1; with 2nd ball of yarn, p1, k1, yo, k3, k3tog, k3, yo, k5.

ROW 23 P1, yo, p3, p3tog, p3, yo, p5, k2tog; with 2nd ball of yarn, ssk, p4, p2tog, p3, [yo, p1] twice, p2, p2tog.

ROW 24 K2tog, k3, [yo, k1] twice, k2, k2tog, k4, p1; with 2nd ball of yarn, p1, k5, yo, k3, k3tog, k3, yo, k1.

ROW 25 P2, yo, p3, p3tog, p3, yo, p4, k2tog; with 2nd ball of yarn, ssk, p3, p2tog, p3, [yo, p1] twice, p2, p2tog, p1, work to end.

ROW 26 K1, p8, k1, k2tog, k3, [yo, k1] twice, k2, k2tog, k3, p1; with 2nd ball of yarn, p1, k4, yo, k3, k3tog, k3, yo, k2.

ROW 27 P2, p2tog, p3, [yo, p1] twice, p2, p2tog, p2, k2tog; with 2nd ball of yarn, ssk, p3, yo, p3, p3tog, p3, yo, p3.

ROW 28 K3, yo, k3, k3tog, k3, yo, k3, p1; with 2nd ball of yarn, p1, k2, k2tog, k3, [yo, k1] twice, k2, k2tog, k2.

ROW 29 P3, p2tog, p3, [yo, p1] twice, p2, p2tog, p1, k2tog; with 2nd ball of yarn, ssk, p2, yo, p3, p3tog, p3, yo, p4.

ROW 30 K1, p4, k5, yo, k3, k3tog, k3, yo, k2, p1; with 2nd ball of yarn, p1, k1, k2tog, k3, [yo, k1] twice, k2, k2tog, k3, work to end.

ROW 31 P2tog, p2, [yo, p1] twice, p2, p3tog, p3, yo, p1, k2tog; with 2nd ball of yarn, ssk, p6, yo, p3, p2tog, p4, work to end.

ROW 32 K4, k2tog, k3, yo, k6, p1; with 2nd ball of yarn, p1, k1, yo, k3, k3tog, k3, [yo, k1] twice, k2, k2tog.

ROW 33 P1, p2tog, p2, [yo, p1] twice, p3, p3tog, p3, yo, k2tog; with 2nd ball of yarn, ssk, p5, yo, p3, p3tog, p3, yo, p1.

ROW 34 K1, yo, k3, k3tog, k3, yo, k5, p1; with 2nd ball of yarn, p1, yo, k3, k3tog, k3, [yo, k1] twice, k1, k2tog, k1.

ROW 35 P2, yo, p3, p3tog, p3, yo, p4, k2tog; with 2nd ball of yarn, ssk, p3, p3tog, p3, [yo, p1] twice, p4.

ROW 36 K5, [yo, k1] twice, k3, k3tog, k3, p1; with 2nd ball of yarn, p1, k4, yo, k3, k3tog, k3, yo, k2.

Work even in pats as established, if necessary, until armhole measures same as back to beg of shoulder shaping. Shape shoulder as for back.

SLEEVES

Cast on 60 (60, 64, 68, 72) sts. Knit 2 rows. Then, beg with a k row, work in St st for 10 rows.

SHAPE CAP

Bind off 4 (4, 4, 5, 5) sts at beg of next 2 rows.

DEC ROW (RS) K1, ssk, k to last 3 sts, k2tog, k1.

Rep dec row every other row 10 (10, 12, 12, 13, 15) times more, then every 4th row once. Bind off 3 sts at beg of next 4 rows. Bind off rem 16 sts.

FINISHING

Block pieces to measurements. Sew shoulder seams. Sew sleeves into armholes. Sew side and sleeve seams.

NECK TRIM

With circular needle, pick up and k 40 sts along back neck and 56 (56, 60, 62, 66) sts along front neck edge. Purl 1 rnd. Bind off knitwise. ✷

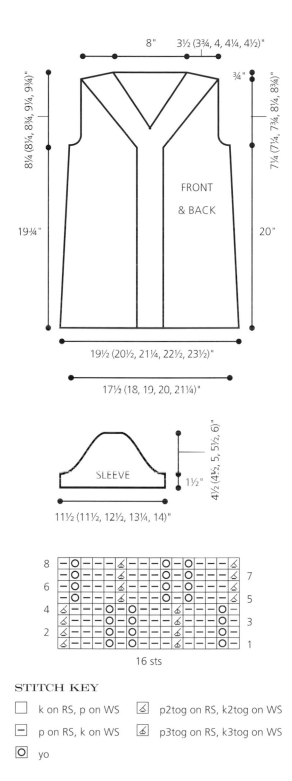

8"   3½ (3¾, 4, 4¼, 4½)"

¾"

8¼ (8¼, 8¾, 9¼, 9¾)"

7¼ (7¼, 7¾, 8¼, 8¾)"

19-¼"   20"

FRONT
& BACK

19½ (20½, 21¼, 22½, 23½)"

17½ (18, 19, 20, 21¼)"

SLEEVE

4½ (4½, 5, 5½, 6)"

1½"

11½ (11½, 12½, 13¼, 14)"

16 sts

STITCH KEY

	k on RS, p on WS		p2tog on RS, k2tog on WS
	p on RS, k on WS		p3tog on RS, k3tog on WS
O	yo		

edgewater shawl

DESIGNED BY
TABETHA HEDRICK
◼◼◻◻

Short-row shaping and
a cable-and-eyelet
border transform a simple
stockinette shawl
into a charming,
one-of-a-kind design.

FINISHED MEASUREMENTS
WINGSPAN Approximately
60"/152.5cm
**LENGTH FROM NECK TO
LONGEST POINT**
Approximately 16"/40.5cm

YARN & NOTIONS
2 hanks *Sabine* in color #13 Acadia

US 8 (5mm) circular needle,
32"(80cm) long, *or size used to
obtain gauge*

Cable needle

GAUGES
18 sts and 31 rows after
blocking = 4"/10cm in St st with
US 8 (5mm) needle.

20 sts and 27 rows after
blocking = 4"/10cm in border pat,
measured lengthwise at the cable
with US 8 (5mm) needle.
Take time to check your gauges.

GLOSSARY
6-ST LC Sl 3 sts to cn and hold to *front*, k3, k3 from cn.

BORDER PAT
(multiple of 19 sts plus 11)
ROW 1 (RS) Sl 1, *k2, yo, k5, k2tog, p2, k6, p2; rep from * to last 10 sts, k2, yo, k5, k2tog, k1.
ROW 2 Sl 1, p2tog, p6, yo, p1, *k2, p6, k2, p2tog, p6, yo, p1; rep from * to last st, p1.
ROW 3 Sl 1, *k3, yo, k4, k2tog, p2, k6, p2; rep from * to last 10 sts, k3, yo, k4, k2tog, k1.
ROW 4 Sl 1, p2tog, p5, yo, p2, *k2, p6, k2, p2tog, p5, yo, p2; rep from * to last st, p1.
ROW 5 Sl 1, *k4, yo, k3, k2tog, p2, 6-st LC, p2; rep from * to last 10 sts, k4, yo, k3, k2tog, k1.
ROW 6 Sl 1, p2tog, p4, yo, p3, *k2, p6, k2, p2tog, p4, yo, p3; rep from * to last st, p1.
ROW 7 Sl 1, k5, yo, k2, k2tog, p2, k6, p2; rep from * to last 10 sts, k5, yo, k2, k2tog, k1.
ROW 8 Sl 1, p2tog, p3, yo, p4, *k2, p6, k2, p2tog, p3, yo, p4; rep from * to last st, p1.
ROW 9 Sl 1, *k6, yo, k1, k2tog, p2, k6, p2; rep from * to last 10 sts, k6, yo, k1, k2tog, k1.
ROW 10 Sl 1, p2tog, p2, yo, p5, *k2, p6, k2, p2tog, p2, yo, p5; rep from * to last st, p1.
ROW 11 Sl 1, *k9, p2, k6, p2; rep from * to last 10 sts, k10.
ROW 12 Sl 1, p9, *k2, p6, k2, p9; rep from * to last st, p1.

NOTES
1) While gauge is not critical to this piece, changing it does affect the amount of yarn used. Adjust this in your planning.
2) Border can be worked using the chart OR the text.
3) Slip sts purlwise with yarn to the WS of the shawl.
4) Shawl body is shaped with short rows.
5) Circular needle is used to accommodate large number of sts. Do not join.

edgewater shawl

BORDER
Cast on 334 sts.

BEGIN BORDER PAT CHART
ROW 1 (RS) Work first st of chart, work 19-st rep 17 times across, work to end of chart.
ROW 2 Work to rep line, work 19-st rep 17 times across, work last st of chart.
Cont in this way until row 12 is complete. Rep rows 1–12 once more.
Knit 6 rows.

SHAWL BODY
NEXT ROW (RS) K170, turn.
ROW 2 P6, turn.
ROW 3 K5, ssk, k3, turn.
ROW 4 P8, p2tog, p3, turn.
ROW 5 K until 1 st rem before the gap, ssk, k3, turn.
ROW 6 P until 1 st rem before the gap, p2tog, p3, turn.
Rep rows 5 and 6 until all sts have been worked—252 sts rem.
Knit 4 rows over all sts.
Bind off loosely.

FINISHING
Block piece to measurements and let air dry completely. ✳

Stitch Key

☐	k on RS, p on WS	╱	k2tog
⊟	p on RS, k on WS	O	yo
⩗	slip 1		6-st LC

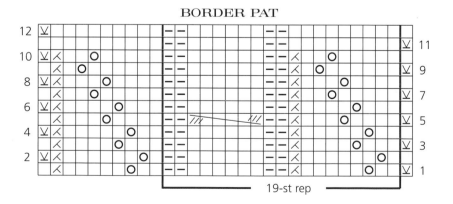

BORDER PAT

19-st rep

maryville cardigan

DESIGNED BY
LOIS S. YOUNG
◼◼◼▢

A vintage-inspired cardigan plays happily with color, as stripes along the bottom, cuffs, and buttonband echo the fancifully patterned yoke.

SIZES
XS (S, M, L, XL)
Shown in S.

FINISHED MEASUREMENTS
BUST (CLOSED) 34 (37, 41, 44¾, 49)"/86.5 (94, 104, 113.5, 125.5)cm
LENGTH 22½ (23, 23½, 24½, 25½)"/57 (58.5, 59.5, 62, 64.5)cm
UPPER ARM 13½ (14½, 15½, 16½, 17½)"/34 (37, 39.5, 42, 44.5)cm

YARN & NOTIONS
8 (9, 10, 12, 13) hanks *Tenzing* in color #07 Crimson (MC)
1 (1, 1, 2, 2) hanks each in colors #05 Arctic River (A) and #09 Alfalfa (B)

US 6 (4mm) circular needle, 29"/70cm long, and 3 straight needles *or size used to obtain gauge*

Nine ⅝"/16mm buttons (three each in red, blue, and green)

GAUGE
25 sts and 32 rows = 4"/10cm in St st with size 6 (4mm) circular needle.
Take time to check your gauge.

GLOSSARY
K2, P2 RIB (FOR SLEEVE)
ROW 1 (RS) K2, *p2, k2; rep from * to end.
ROW 2 P2, *k2, p2; rep from * to end.
Rep rows 1 and 2 for k2, p2 rib for sleeve.

K2, P2 RIB (FOR BODY)
ROW 1 (RS) K3, *p2, k2; rep from *, end k1.
ROW 2 P3, *k2, p2; rep from *, end p1.
Rep rows 1 and 2 for k2, p2 rib for body.

NOTE
Make sleeves first and set aside to be joined with body while working the yoke.

SLEEVES
With straight needles and A, cast on 46 (46, 46, 50, 54) sts. Work k2, p2 rib and stripe pat as foll: 2 rows A, 2 rows MC, and 2 rows B. With MC only, cont in rib until piece measures 3"/7.5cm from beg, end with a WS row.
NEXT (INC) ROW (RS) K5 (5, 5, 3, 5), [M1, k4 (4, 4, 5, 5)] 9 times, M1, k5 (5, 5, 2, 4)—56 (56, 56, 60, 64) sts.
Purl next row. Work in St st (k on RS, p on WS) for 4 rows, end with a WS row.
NEXT (INC) ROW (RS) K1 (selvage st), M1, k to last st, M1, k1 (selvage st).
Rep inc row every 4th row 0 (5, 12, 13, 16) times more, then every 6th row 14 (12, 8, 8, 6) times. Work even on 86 (92, 98, 104, 110) sts until piece measures 17½ (17½, 17½, 18, 18)"/44.5 (44.5, 44.5, 45.5, 45.5)cm from beg, end with a WS row. Bind off 10 (12, 12, 13, 14) sts at beg of next 2 rows. Leave rem 66 (68, 74, 78, 82) sts on spare needle.

BODY
With circular needle and A, cast on 208 (224, 248, 272, 300) sts. Do not join. Work back and forth in k2, p2 rib and stripe pat as foll: 2 rows A, 2 rows MC, and 2 rows B. With MC only, cont in rib pat until piece measures 2½"/6.5cm from beg, end with a WS row. Cont in St st and work even until piece measures 13 (13, 13, 13½, 14)"/33 (33, 33, 34, 35.5)cm from beg, end with a RS row.

SEPARATE FOR FRONTS AND BACK
NEXT ROW (WS) P 42 (45, 51, 56, 62) sts (left front), bind off next 20 (22, 22, 24, 26) sts, p until there are 84 (90, 102,

maryville cardigan

112, 124) sts on needle (back), bind off next 20 (22, 22, 24, 26) sts, p until there are 42 (45, 51, 56, 62) sts on needle (right front).

YOKE

NEXT ROW (RS) With circular needle and MC, k 42 (45, 51, 56, 62) sts (right front), k 66 (68, 74, 78, 82) sts of first sleeve, k 84 (90, 102, 112, 124) sts (back), k 66 (68, 74, 78, 82) sts of 2nd sleeve, k 42 (45, 51, 56, 62) sts (left front)—300 (316, 352, 380, 412) sts. Beg with a purl row, cont in St st for 9 (13, 15, 19, 23) rows, inc (dec, dec, dec, dec) 1 (3, 3, 7, 3) sts evenly spaced across last row and end with a WS row—301 (313, 349, 373, 409) sts.

BEG CHART PAT 1

ROW 1 (RS) Work to rep line, work 6-st rep 49 (51, 57, 61, 67) times, work to end. Cont in this way until row 6 is complete, then rep rows 1–6 once more, then rows 1–3 once. Work in stripe pat as foll: 3 rows MC, 1 row B, 1 row MC, 1 row A, and 1 row MC.

DEC ROW 1 (RS) With MC, k4, *k2tog, k1; rep from * to last 6 sts, end k2tog, k4—203 (211, 235, 251, 275) sts. With MC, purl next row.

BEG CHART PAT 2

ROW 1 (RS) Beg chart where indicated for size being made and work to rep line, work 6-st rep 33 (34, 38, 41, 45) times, work to end for size being made. Cont in this way until row 6 is complete, then rep rows 1–3 once more. Work in stripe pat as foll: 3 rows MC, 1 row A, 1 row MC, 1 row B, and 1 row MC.

DEC ROW 2 (RS) With MC, k2tog, k1, *k2tog, k2; rep from * to last 4 sts, end [k2tog] twice—151 (157, 175, 187, 205) sts. With MC, purl next row.

BEG CHART PAT 1

ROW 1 (RS) Work to rep line, work 6-st rep 24 (25, 28, 30, 33) times, work to end. Work to row 6, end with a WS row. Work in stripe pat as foll: 3 rows MC, 1 row A, 1 row MC, 1 row B, and 1 row MC, end with a RS row.

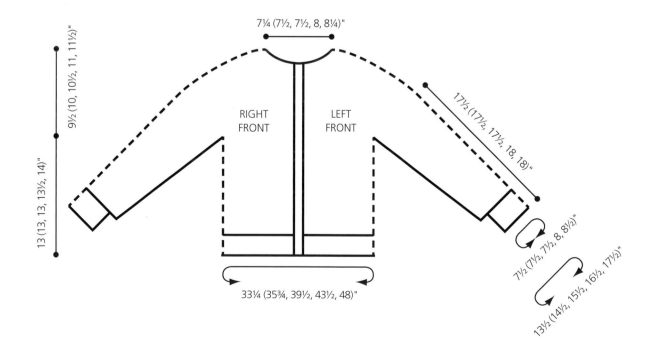

7¼ (7½, 7½, 8, 8¼)"

9½ (10, 10½, 11, 11½)"

13 (13, 13, 13½, 14)"

RIGHT FRONT

LEFT FRONT

17½ (17½, 17½, 18, 18)"

7½ (7½, 7½, 8, 8½)"

13½ (14½, 15½, 16½, 17½)"

33¼ (35¾, 39½, 43½, 48)"

maryville cardigan

DEC ROW 3 (WS) With MC, p1 (4, 3, 4, 5), *[p2tog] twice, p1; rep from *, end p0 (3, 2, 3, 5)—91 (97, 107, 115, 127) sts.

For sizes XS (S) only:
With MC, work row 1 of k2, p2 rib for body, inc (dec) 1 st in center of back neck—92 (96) sts.

For size M only:
With MC, work even for 2 rows, end with a WS row.
DEC ROW 4 (RS) [K7, k2tog] 11 times, end k8—96 sts. Purl next row.

For size L only:
With MC, work even for 2 rows, end with a WS row.
DEC ROW 4 (RS) K2, [k5, k2tog] 15 times, end k8—100 sts. Purl next row.

For size XL only:
With MC, work even for 2 rows, end with a WS row.
DEC ROW 4 (RS) K4, [k3, k2tog] 23 times, end k8—104 sts. Purl next row.

For all sizes:
Beg with row 2 (2, 1, 1, 1), work in k2, p2 rib for body for 6 (6, 7, 7, 7) rows. Bind off loosely in rib.

FINISHING
Block piece to measurements. Sew sleeve seams. Sew underarm seams.

BUTTONBAND
With circular needle, MC and RS facing, beg at top edge of left front, pick up and k 134 (137, 141, 147, 153) sts evenly spaced to lower edge.
NEXT ROW Sl 1 purlwise, k to last st, k1tbl. Rep this row for garter st and work in stripe pat as foll: 1 row MC, 2 rows B, 6 rows MC, 2 rows A, and 1 row MC. Bind off loosely knitwise with MC. Place markers for 9 buttonholes along right front edge, with first marker 1"/2.5cm from lower edge, last marker ½"/13mm from top edge, and 7 markers evenly spaced between.

BUTTONHOLE BAND
With circular needle, MC and RS facing, beg at lower edge of right front, pick up and k 134 (137, 141, 147, 153) sts evenly spaced to top edge. Work as for buttonband until 5 rows of garter st stripe pat (1 row MC, 2 rows B, and 2 rows MC) have been worked, end with a WS row.
NEXT (BUTTONHOLE) ROW (RS) With MC, sl 1 purlwise, [k to marker, yo, k2tog] 9 times, k to last st, k1tbl. Cont to work last 5 rows of garter st stripe pat. Bind off loosely knitwise with MC. Sew on buttons foll color sequence as shown. ✳

CHART 1

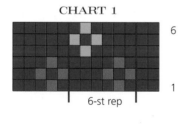

6-st rep

CHART 2

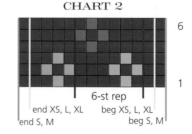

6-st rep

end XS, L, XL   beg XS, L, XL
end S, M   beg S, M

COLOR KEY

■ MC
■ A
■ B

williston hat

DESIGNED BY
NADIA ELGAWARSHA

A chunky yarn, wide ribbed brim, and dense honeycomb pattern formed with cables make a classic go-to topper for the coldest days of winter.

SIZE
One Size: Adult Woman

FINISHED MEASUREMENTS
BRIM CIRCUMFERENCE 18"/45.5cm
LENGTH 10"/25.5cm

YARN & NOTIONS
1 hank *Herriot Great* each in color
#105 Rosewood (A) and
#107 Cornflower (B)

US 5 and 9 (3.75 and 5.5mm)
double-pointed needles (set of 5)
or *sizes used to obtain gauge*

Stitch markers, cable needle

GAUGE
28 sts and 22 rnds = 4"/10cm
in pat st with larger needles.
Take time to check your gauge.

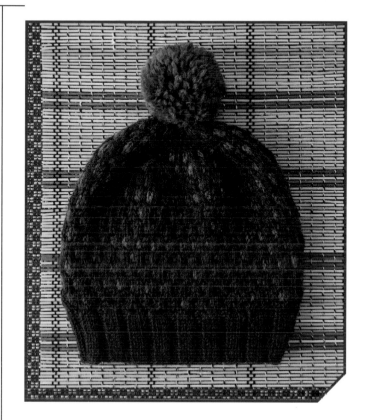

GLOSSARY
2-ST RC Sl 1 st to cn and hold to *back*, k1, k1 from cn.
2-ST LC Sl 1 st to cn and hold to *front*, k1, k1 from cn.

PATTERN STITCH
(multiple of 4 sts)
RND 1 *K1 B, k2 A, k1 B; rep from * around.
RND 2 *2-st LC, 2-st RC; rep from * around.
RND 3 *K1 A, k2 B, k1 A; rep from * around.
RND 4 Rep rnd 3.
RND 5 *2-st RC, 2-st LC; rep from * around.
RND 6 Rep rnd 1.
Rep rows 1–6 for pat st.

HAT
With smaller dpns and A, cast on 100 sts. Join, being careful not to twist sts, and place marker for beg of rnd.

williston hat

NEXT RND *K3, p2; rep from * around.
Rep last rnd for rib until piece measures 2"/5cm from beg.
NEXT (INC) RND *K3, M1, p2, M1; rep from * around—140 sts.

BEGIN PATTERN ST
Work in pat st until piece measures approx 8"/20.5cm from beg, end with a row 6.

SHAPE CROWN
RND 1 (DEC) *[K1 B, k2 A, k2tog B, k2 A, k1 B] twice, k1 B, k2 A, k1 B; rep from * 6 times more—126 sts.
RND 2 (DEC) *[2-st RC, 2-st LC, SK2P A] twice, 2-st RC, 2-st LC; rep from * 6 times more—98 sts.
RND 3 *K1 A, [k2 B, k3 A] twice, k2 B, k1 A; rep from * 6 times more.

RND 4 (DEC) *K1 A, [k2 B, k1 A, k2tog A] twice, k2 B, k1 A; rep from * 6 times more—84 sts.
RND 5 [2-st LC, 2-st RC] 21 times around.
RND 6 (DEC) *K1 B, k2 A, [k2tog B, k2 A] twice, k1 B; rep from * 6 times more—70 sts.
RND 7 (DEC) [K1 B, k2 A, k2tog B, SKP B, k2 A, k1 B] 7 times around—56 sts.
RND 8 [2-st RC, 2-st LC] 14 times around.
RND 9 (DEC) [K1 A, k2tog B, k1 A] 14 times around—42 sts.
RND 10 (DEC) [SK2P A] 14 times around—14 sts.
Break yarn, leaving a long tail. Thread tail through open sts and pull tight to close.

FINISHING
Make a 3"/7.5cm pompom with B and sew to top of hat.✳

spring hill scarf

DESIGNED BY
LISA CRAIG

◼◼◻◻

A pretty pastel scarf knit in trinity stitch comes to life with an unexpected embellishment: fringe made of flowers.

FINISHED MEASUREMENTS
Approximately 5 x 42"/12.5 x 106.5cm

YARN & NOTIONS
2 hanks *Moonshine* in color #04 Seaside

US 7 (4.5mm) straight needles

US 6 (4mm) double-pointed needles (set of 2) *or sizes used to obtain gauge*

Tapestry needle

GAUGE
24 sts and 28 rows = 4"/10cm in trinity st with larger needles. *Take time to check your gauge.*

GLOSSARY
TRINITY STITCH
(multiple of 4 sts)
ROW 1 (RS) Purl.
ROW 2 *(K1, p1, k1) into next st, p3tog; rep from * to end.
ROW 3 Purl.
ROW 4 *P3tog, (k1, p1, k1) into next st; rep from * to end.
Rep rows 1–4 for trinity st.

SCARF
With larger needles, cast on 10 sts.
Knit 2 rows.
NEXT (INC) ROW (RS) K1, M1, k to last st, M1, k1—2 sts inc'd.
Cont in garter st (k every row), rep inc row every 4th row 8 times more—28 sts.
NEXT (INC) ROW (WS) K5, M1, [k6, M1] 3 times, M1, k5—32 sts.

69

spring hill scarf

BEGIN TRINITY ST
NEXT ROW (RS) K2, work row 1 of trinity st to last 2 sts, k2.
Keeping first and last 2 sts of each row in garter st (k every row), cont in trinity st until piece measures approx 38"/96.5cm from beg, end with a RS row.
NEXT ROW (WS) [K5, k2tog] 4 times, k4—28 sts.
NEXT (DEC) ROW (RS) K1, k2tog, k to last 3 sts, k2tog, k1—2 sts dec'd.
Cont in garter st, rep dec row every 4th row 7 times more—12 sts.
NEXT ROW (WS) K1, k2tog, k to last 3 sts, k2tog, k1—10 sts.
Knit 2 rows. Bind off.

LARGE FLOWER (MAKE 2)
With larger needles, cast on 4 sts.
ROW 1 (WS) Knit.
ROW 2 Cast on 3 sts, k to end of row—7 sts.
ROWS 3, 4, AND 5 Knit.
ROW 6 Sl 1, k3, pass 2nd, 3rd, and 4th sts over sl st, k3—4 sts.
Rep rows 1–6 five times more. Bind off and break yarn, leaving a long tail.
Thread tail through tapestry needle and draw through straight end of flower. Pull firmly and secure.
Sew cast-on edge to bound-off edge.
Sew 1 flower to each end of scarf, using photo as guide.

SMALL FLOWER (MAKE 10)
With smaller needles, cast on 3 sts.
ROW 1 Knit.
ROW 2 Cast on 3 sts, k to end of row—6 sts.
ROWS 3, 4, AND 5 Knit.
ROW 6 Sl 1, k3, pass 2nd, 3rd, and 4th sts over sl st, k3—3 sts.
Rep rows 1–6 five times more. Bind off and break yarn, leaving a long tail.
Complete as for large flower.

I-CORD
Make 10 I-cords, 2 each 6"/15cm long, 4 each 4" and 2"/10cm and 2.5cm long, as foll:
With dpn, cast on 2 sts, *k2, slide sts to opposite end of needle to work next row from the RS, pulling yarn firmly across back of work; rep from * to desired length.
Break yarn, leaving a long tail. Thread tail through open sts to fasten off cord.

FINISHING
Using photo as guide, sew 1 small flower to 1 end of each cord. Sew longest cord to center of each point of scarf. Sew shortest cords to outside edge of each end of scarf.
Sew 2 rem cords evenly spaced between short and long cords on each end. ✲

county line vest

DESIGNED BY
THERESA SCHABES
◼◼◼▢

With creative styling, a menswear-inspired plaid vest can inspire a tomboy look or bring a fresh sense of contrast to a more feminine ensemble.

SIZES
S (M, L, 1X, 2X, 3X)
Shown in S.

FINISHED MEASUREMENTS
BUST 34 (36½, 39, 40½, 46, 48)"/86 (92.5, 99, 103, 117, 122)cm
LENGTH 23¾ (23¾, 24¼, 24½, 25, 25¼)"/60 (60, 61.5, 62, 63.5, 64)cm

YARN & NOTIONS
1 (1, 2, 2, 2, 2) balls *Findley DK* in color #06 Rappahannock (A)

1 (1, 2, 2, 2, 2) balls *Findley* each in colors #19 Rappahannock (B), #24 Snowy Skies (C), and #29 Greengage (D)

US 5 (3.75mm) circular needle, 16"/40cm long, and straight needles *or size used to obtain gauge*

Size F/5 (3.75mm) crochet hook, bobbins, stitch markers

GAUGE
21 sts and 33 rows = 4"/10cm in St st and plaid pat foll chart with 2 strands of *Findley* held tog and US 5 (3.75 mm) needles.
Take time to check your gauge.

NOTES
1) All ribbed borders are worked using 1 strand of *Findley DK* (A). The body of the garment is worked in plaid pat foll chart, using 2 strands of B, C, or D held tog or 1 strand B and 1 strand C held tog. Wind yarn onto bobbins and do not strand the yarn across back of work when changing colors for each color block. Twist yarn tog at the color changes to avoid holes in work.
2) All vertical lines worked in 2 strands of D are worked into the purl line sts using a crochet hook after the pieces are knit.

BACK
With 1 strand A, cast on 94 (98, 102, 110, 122, 126) sts.
ROW 1 (RS) K3, *p2, k2; rep from *, end last rep k3.
ROW 2 P1, *k2, p2; rep from *, end last rep p3.
Rep these 2 rows for k2, p2 rib for 1"/2.5cm, dec 2 (0, 0, 2, 2, 0) sts on the last WS row—92 (98, 102, 108, 120, 126) sts.

BEGIN CHART
NOTE St 1 and st 20 of chart are the selvage sts.
ROW 1 (RS) K1 (selvage st), beg with st 2 (17, 15, 12, 15, 12) of chart, work to end of rep line, then work the 18-st rep 4 (5, 5, 5, 6, 6) times more, rep sts 2–19 (2–4, 2–6, 2–9, 2–6, 2–9) once more, k1 (selvage st). Cont to work chart in this way until row 26 is complete. Rep rows 1–26 until piece measures 3½"/9cm from beg.

SHAPE WAIST
DEC ROW (RS) K1, ssk, work chart pat to last 3 sts, k2tog, k1. Rep dec row every 8th row 4 times more—82 (88, 92, 98, 110, 116) sts. Work even until piece measures 9"/23cm from beg.
INC ROW (RS) K1, kfb, work chart pat to last 2 sts, kfb, k1. Rep inc row every 8th row 4 times more—92 (98, 102, 108, 120, 126) sts. Work even until piece measures 14"/35.5cm from beg.

SHAPE ARMHOLE
Bind off 6 (7, 7, 7, 8, 9) sts at beg of next 2 rows, 2 sts at beg of next 6 rows.
DEC ROW (RS) K1, ssk, work pat to last 3 sts, k2tog, k1. Rep dec row every other row 3 (4, 4, 5, 5, 7) times more, then every 4th row 2 (3, 3, 3, 3, 3) times—56 (56, 60, 64, 74, 74) sts.

county line vest

Work even until armhole measures 8 (8, 8½, 8¾, 9¼, 9½)"/20.5 (20.5, 21.5, 22, 23.5, 24)cm. Place markers (pm) to mark center 12 (12, 12, 16, 18, 18) sts.

SHAPE NECK
NEXT ROW (RS) Work to center marked sts, join new yarn if necessary and bind off center 12 (12, 12, 16, 18, 18) sts, work to end. Working both sides at once, bind off 6 sts from each neck edge once, 3 sts once, 2 sts once, and 1 st once, AT THE SAME TIME, when armhole measures 9 (9, 9½, 9¾, 10¼, 10½)"/23 (23, 24, 25, 26, 26.5)cm, shape shoulders by binding off 5 (5, 6, 6, 6, 6) sts from each armhole edge once, 3 (3, 3, 3, 5, 5) sts once, and 2 (2, 3, 3, 5, 5) sts once.

FRONT
Work as for back, including armhole shaping, until armhole measures 6 (6, 6½, 6¾, 7¼, 7½)"/15 (15, 16.5, 17, 18.5, 19)cm. Pm to mark center 8 (8, 8, 12, 14, 14) sts.

SHAPE NECK
NEXT ROW (RS) Work to center marked sts, join new yarn if necessary and bind off center 8 (8, 8, 12, 14, 14) sts, work to end. Working both sides at once, bind off 3 sts from each neck edge once, 2 sts twice, 1 st every other row 5 times, 1 st every 4th row twice, AT THE SAME TIME, when armhole measures same as back, bind off 5 (5, 6, 6, 6, 6) sts from each shoulder edge once, 3 (3, 3, 3, 5, 5) sts once, and 2 (2, 3, 3, 5, 5) sts once.

To work the vertical lines in color D, using 2 strands of D and crochet hook and holding the yarn at the WS of work, put a loop on hook and insert hook from RS to WS in the first purl bar at the lower edge, pull yarn through the loop from the WS to the RS and cont in this way (working loosely so that the chains don't alter the length of the fabric) until a chain is worked in every purl bump along one purl line. Fasten off at top of piece. Work other vertical-line chains in same way.
Sew shoulder seams and side seams.

ARMHOLE TRIMS
With 1 strand A and circular needle, pick up and k 100 (100, 104, 108, 116, 120) sts evenly around armhole. Join and pm to work in rnds.
RND 1 *K2, p2; rep from * around. Cont in k2, p2 rib for 1"/2.5cm. Bind off in rib.

NECKBAND
With 1 strand A and circular needle, pick up and k 100 (100, 100, 108, 112, 112) sts evenly around neck edge. Join and pm to work in rnds. Work in k2, p2 rib in rnds as on armhole for 1"/2.5cm. Bind off in rib. Block to measurements. ✳

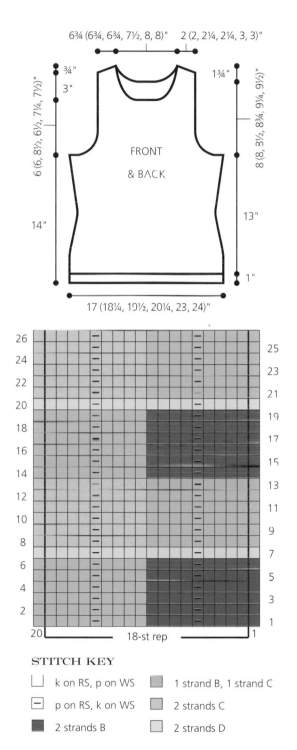

6¾ (6¾, 6¾, 7½, 8, 8)"   2 (2, 2¼, 2¼, 3, 3)"

¾"

3"

1¾"

6 (6, 8½, 6½, 7¼, 7½)"

FRONT
& BACK

8 (8, 8½, 3½, 8¾, 9¼, 9½)"

14"

13"

1"

17 (18¼, 19½, 20¼, 23, 24)"

18-st rep

STITCH KEY

⬜ k on RS, p on WS   🟦 1 strand B, 1 strand C

⊟ p on RS, k on WS   🟦 2 strands C

🟦 2 strands B   ⬜ 2 strands D

hopewell hat and mitts

DESIGNED BY
ALISON GREEN
■■■▭

The hat's single seed stitch
and cable panel is echoed
on each mitt for a matching
set that'll keep you feeling
toasty and looking subtly
sophisticated.

SIZES
HAT S (M, L)
Shown in S.

MITTS One size. Adult Woman

FINISHED MEASUREMENTS
HAT
BRIM CIRCUMFERENCE 18½ (20,
20½)"/47(51, 54.5)cm
LENGTH 8"/20.5cm

MITTS
HAND CIRCUMFERENCE 7"/18cm
LENGTH 10"/25.5cm

YARN & NOTIONS
1 hank *Herriot Heathers* in color
#103 Dark Harbor

US 3 and 6 (3.25 and 4mm) circular
needles, 16"/40cm long

US 3 and 6 (3.25 and 4mm)
double-pointed needles *or sizes
used to obtain gauge*

Stitch markers, cable needle,
scrap yarn

GAUGE
32 sts and 36 rnds = 4"/10cm
in cable panel with larger needles.
Take time to check your gauge.

GLOSSARY
SEED STITCH
RND 1 *K1, p1; rep from * to end.
RND 2 K the purl sts and p the knit sts.
Rep rnd 2 for seed st.

3-ST RC Sl 1 st to cn and hold to *back*, k2, k1 from cn.
3-ST LC Sl 2 sts to cn and hold to *front*, k1, k2 from cn.
3-ST RPC Sl 1 st to cn and hold to *back*, k2, p1 from cn.
3-ST LPC Sl 2 sts to cn and hold to *front*, p1, k2 from cn.
4-ST LC Sl 2 sts to cn and hold to *front*, k2, k2 from cn.
4-ST RPC Sl 2 sts to cn and hold to *back*, k2, p2 from cn.
4-ST LPC Sl 2 sts to cn and hold to *front*, p2, k2 from cn.

HAT
With smaller circular needle, cast on 120 (130, 140) sts.
Join, being careful not to twist sts, and place marker (pm)
for beg of rnd.

BRIM
Work in seed st for 6 rnds. Knit 1 rnd, purl 1 rnd.
Change to larger needle.
NEXT (INC) RND K6, M1, k4, M1, k2, M1, k4, M1, k6, pm,
k to end of rnd—124 (134, 144) sts.

BEGIN CABLE CHART
NEXT RND Work rnd 1 of cable chart over 26 sts, sl marker,
k to end.
Cont in this way until rnd 24 of chart is complete, then rep
rnds 1–24 (23, 21) once more.

SHAPE CROWN
NOTE Change to dpns when sts no longer fit comfortably on
circular needle.
Move end-of-rnd marker 0 (2, 3) sts to the right.

For size L only:
NEXT (DEC) RND Ssk, k1, work next rnd of cable chart over 26
sts, k1, k2tog, [ssk, k24, k2tog] 4 times—134 sts.
Work 1 rnd even.

For sizes M and L only:
NEXT (DEC) RND Ssk, k1, work next rnd of cable chart over 26
sts, k1, k2tog, [ssk, k22, k2tog] 4 times—124 sts.
Work 1 rnd even.

hopewell hat and mitts

For all sizes:

BEGIN CABLE DEC CHART

NEXT (DEC) RND Work rnd 1 of cable dec chart to marker, sl marker, [ssk, k20, k2tog, pm] 4 times around—114 sts.

NEXT RND Work next rnd of cable dec chart, k to end.

NEXT (DEC) RND Work next rnd of cable dec chart to marker, sl marker [ssk, k to 2 sts before next marker, k2tog, sl marker] 4 times around—104 sts.

NEXT RND Work next rnd of cable dec chart, k to end. Cont in this way, working dec rnd every other rnd, until rnd 19 of cable dec chart is complete—20 sts.

NEXT RND [Ssk, k2tog] 5 times around—10 sts.

Cut yarn, leaving a long tail. Thread tail through open sts and fasten off.

FINISHING

Wash and gently block. ✳

CABLE DEC CHART

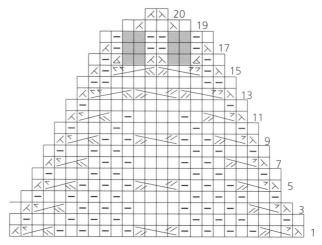

CABLE CHART

STITCH KEY

☐	k on RS, p on WS
⊟	p on RS, k on WS
⟋	k2tog
⟍	SKP
⟋	p2tog
▩	no stitch
	3-st RC
	3-st LC
	3-st RPC
	3-st LPC
	4-st LC
	4-st RPC
	4-st LPC

hopewell hat and mitts

MITTS

RIGHT MITT

With US 3 (3.25 mm) dpns, cast on 44 sts. Join, being careful not to twist sts, and pm for beg of rnd.

CUFF

Work in seed st for 6 rnds. Knit 1 rnd, purl 1 rnd, Change to larger needle.

NEXT (INC) RND K6, M1, k4, M1, k2, M1, k4, M1, k6, pm, k to end of rnd—48 sts.

BEGIN CABLE CHART

NEXT RND Work rnd 1 of cable chart over 26 sts, sl marker, k to end.

Cont in this way until rnd 24 of chart is complete. Rep rnds 1–24 until piece measures 4½"/11.5cm from beg.

THUMB GUSSET

NEXT (INC) RND Work chart rnd to marker, sl marker, M1, pm, k to end—49 sts.

Work 2 rnds even.

NEXT RND Work to marker, sl marker, M1L, k1, M1R, sl marker, k to end—2 sts inc'd.

Work 2 rnds even.

Rep last 3 rnds 6 times more—63 sts.

NEXT RND Work to marker, sl marker, place 15 gusset sts on scrap yarn, removing next marker, k to end—48 sts.

Cont to work in pat as established until piece measures approx 9"/23cm from beg, end with a chart rnd 24. (Rnds 1–24 have been worked a total of 3 times.)

NEXT (DEC) RND K5, ssk, k3, ssk, k2, k2tog, k3, k2tog, k to end—44 sts.

Change to smaller needles.

Purl 1 rnd, knit 1 rnd.

Work in seed st for 6 rnds. Bind off.

THUMB

Place 15 sts from scrap yarn on needles.

Pick up and k 2 sts in gap of thumb gusset, k15, k1 (the first st you picked up)—17 sts. Pm for beg of rnd.

NEXT (DEC) RND K2tog, k to last 2 sts, ssk—15 sts.

NEXT RND K15.

Rep last rnd until thumb measures 1"/2.5cm.

Purl 1 rnd. Bind off.

LEFT MITT

Work as for right mitt to thumb gusset.

THUMB GUSSET

NEXT (INC) RND M1, pm, work in pat to end—49 sts.

Work 2 rnds even.

NEXT (INC) RND M1L, k1, M1R, sl marker, work in pat to end—2 sts inc'd.

Work 2 rnds even.

Rep last 3 rnds 6 times more—63 sts.

NEXT RND Place 15 gusset sts on scrap yarn, removing marker, work to end of rnd—48 sts.

Complete as for right mitt.

FINISHING

Wash and gently block. ✳

cloudcroft pullover

**DESIGNED BY
GALINA CARROLL**
■■■▢

A loose, poncho-like shape, lofty yarn, and puffy pompom ties will make you feel like you're wrapped in a warm winter-white cloud.

SIZES
S (M/L, XL/2X)
Shown in M/L.

FINISHED MEASUREMENTS
BUST (BELOW SLEEVE) 39 (43, 46)"/99 (109, 117)cm
LENGTH 28"/71cm

YARN & NOTIONS
9 (10, 11) balls *Herriot Great* in color #100 Raw White

2 US 10 (6mm) circular needles, each 40"/100cm long

2 each US 8 and 9 (5 and 5.5cm) circular needles, 24 and 40"/60 and 100cm long

US 7 (4.5mm) circular needle, 24"/60cm long, and double-pointed needles (set of 4) *or sizes used to obtain gauge*

Stitch markers

GAUGE
9 sts and 20 rows = 4"/10cm in fisherman's rib with size US 10 (6mm) needles.
Take time to check your gauge.

GLOSSARY
K1B Knit 1 into the row below.
P1B Purl 1 into the row below.

FISHERMAN'S RIB
(in rows, over an even number of sts)
ROW 1 (WS) *K1, p1; rep from * to end.
ROW 2 *K1b, p1; rep from * to end.
Rep row 2 for fisherman's rib in rows.

FISHERMAN'S RIB
(in rnds, over an even number of sts)
RND 1 *K1, p1b; rep from * around.
RND 2 *K1b, p1; rep from * around.
Rep rnds 1 and 2 for fisherman's rib in rnds.

TWISTED CORD
1) Cut 2 strands of yarn 3 times the desired length of cord and knot them together approx 1"/2.5cm from each end.
2) Insert a pencil or knitting needle through one end and anchor the other end of the strands.
3) Turn the strands clockwise until they are tightly twisted.
4) Keeping strands taut, fold piece in half. Remove knitting needle and allow cords to twist onto themselves.

NOTE
When counting rnds or rows in fisherman's rib, each large knit st counts as 2 rows or rnds worked.

SWEATER
With size US 10 (6mm) needle, cast on 44 (48, 52) sts for back. Work in fisherman's rib for 21 rows, end with a WS row. Set piece aside.

FRONT
With 2nd size US 10 (6mm) needle, cast on as for back. Work in fisherman's rib for 11 rows, end with a WS row.

JOIN FRONT AND BACK
NEXT RND Work in pat over 44 (48, 52) sts for front, place marker (pm) for side edge, work in pat over 44 (48, 52) sts for back, pm for beg of rnd—88 (96, 104) sts.
Work in fisherman's rib in the rnd until 40 rnds have been worked from joining of front and back.

cloudcroft pullover

INCREASE FOR SLEEVES
NEXT RND Work in pat over 44 (48, 52) sts for front, sl marker, cast on 44 (48, 48) sts for sleeve, pm, work in pat over 44 (48, 52) sts for back, pm, cast on 44 (48, 48) sts for sleeve—176 (192, 200) sts.

Change to longer size US 9 (5.5mm) needle. Cont in pat over all sts, working 1 rnd of k1, p1 rib over cast-on sleeve sts, then incorporating them into pat. When 40 rnds have been worked since sleeve increase, change to longer size US 8 (5mm) needle. Cont in pat for 20 rnds. Change to size US 7 (4.5mm) circular needle. Cont in pat for 20 rnds.

NECK
NEXT (DEC) RND *K2tog, p2tog; rep from * around—88 (96, 100) sts.

NEXT RND *K1, p1; rep from * around.

Rep last rnd for k1, p1 rib 24 times more. Change to shorter size 8 (5mm) needle and work 5 rnds more in k1, p1 rib. Change to shorter size 9 (5.5mm) needle and work 5 rnds more in k1, p1 rib.

Bind off loosely in rib.

FINISHING
Place markers approx 6"/15cm from top of sleeve opening at front and back side edges. Sew underarm seam to marker.

CUFF
With RS facing and dpns, pick up and k 38 sts around rem sleeve opening. Join and pm for beg of rnd. Work in rnds of k1, p1 rib until cuff measures 4½"/11.5cm.

CORD
Make a twisted cord 40"/101.5cm long. Make 2 pompoms 3½"/9cm in diameter and secure one to each end of cord. Thread cord through dec row at base of neck with pompoms at front, tie in bow. ✳

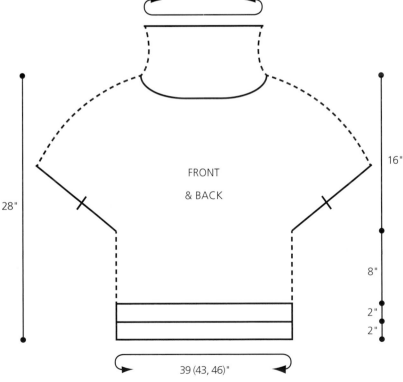

summerdale dress

DESIGNED BY
CAROLINE FRYAR

A flattering pleated skirt and casually wrapped belt help achieve an easy, breezy feel in a versatile warm-weather dress.

SIZES
XS (S, M, L, XL)
Shown in XS.

FINISHED MEASUREMENTS
BUST 31 (34, 37, 40, 43)"/77½ (80, 87½, 95, 102½)cm
LENGTH 36½, (37¼, 38, 38¾, 39½)"/92.5 (94.5, 96.5, 98.5, 100)cm
(**NOTE** Dress is designed to be worn with 0–1"/0–2.5cm positive ease.)

YARN & NOTIONS
3 (3, 3, 3, 3) balls *Findley Dappled* in color #03 Fruits de Fôret

US 4 and 9 (3.5 and 5.5mm) circular needles, 24"/60cm long, *or sizes used to obtain gauge*

Scrap yarn, stitch markers, tapestry needle

GAUGE
24 sts and 40 rows = 4"/10cm after blocking, in St st with smaller needles.
Take time to check your gauge.

GLOSSARY
PLEATED PATTERN
(multiple of 10 sts)
RND 1 *K1, p1, k1, sl 1 wyib, k1, p1, k1, p3; rep from * to end.
RND 2 *K1, p1, k3, p1, k1, p1, sl 1 wyif, p1; rep from * to end.
Rep rnds 1 and 2 for pleated pat.

LINEN STITCH
(over an odd number of sts)
ROW 1 (RS) K1, *sl 1 wyif, k1; rep from * to end.
ROW 2 (WS) K1, p1, *sl 1 wyib, p1; rep from * to last st, k1.
Rep rows 1 and 2 for linen st.

summerdale dress

SEWN BIND-OFF
1) Cut yarn, leaving a tail 3 times the circumference of the skirt hem, and thread through tapestry needle.
2) Insert the needle purlwise through the first 2 sts on knitting needle, and pull tight.
3) Insert tapestry needle knitwise into the first st and pull tight. Drop st from knitting needle.
Rep steps 2 and 3 until all sts have been bound off.

NOTE
Dress is worked from the top down.

BACK NECK
With smaller needles, cast on 48 (48, 51, 51, 54) sts for back neck.
NEXT ROW (WS) P1, place marker (pm), p2 for shoulder, pm, p42 (42, 45, 45, 48), pm, p2 for shoulder, pm, p1.
SET-UP ROW (RS) Sl 1, M1, sl marker, k2, sl marker, M1, k1 (1, 3, 3, 4), [M1, k2] 20 times, k1 (1, 2, 2, 4), M1, sl marker, k2, sl marker, M1, k1—72 (72, 75, 75, 78) sts.
NEXT (INC) ROW (WS) Sl 1, [p to marker, M1, sl marker, p2, sl marker, M1] twice—4 sts inc'd.

NEXT (INC) ROW (RS) Sl 1, [k to marker, M1, sl marker, k2, sl marker, M1] twice—4 sts inc'd.
Rep last 2 rows 6 (7, 7, 8, 9) times more—128 (136, 139, 147, 158) sts.
Work even until shoulder measures 2½ (2¾, 3, 3¼, 3½)"/6.5 (7, 7.5, 8, 9)cm, end with a WS row.

DIVIDE FRONTS AND BACK
NEXT ROW (RS) Sl 1, k15 (17, 17, 19, 21) for left front, join 2nd ball of yarn and bind off 2 shoulder sts, k to next marker, join 3rd ball of yarn and bind off 2 shoulder sts, k to end for right front.
Working 3 sections (left front, right front, and back) at once with 3 balls of yarn, cont in St st, slipping first st of each row on each section, until work measures 7 (7¼, 7½, 7¾, 8)"/18 (18.5, 19, 19.5, 20.5)cm from bound-off edge, end with a WS row.

JOIN FRONTS AND BACK
JOINING RND (RS) Beg with back piece, k92 (96, 99, 103, 110), cast on 6 sts for right underarm, k16 (18, 18, 20, 22) right front sts, cast on 54 (66, 75, 87, 96) sts for center front, k 16 (18, 18, 20, 22) left front sts, cast on 6 sts for left underarm.
Pm for beg of rnd—190 (210, 222, 242, 262) sts.
Work 5 rnds even.

BEGIN BUST DART SHAPING
For sizes XS (S) only:
NEXT (SET-UP) RND K31 (3), place dart marker, k30 (32), place dart marker, k66 (72), place dart marker, k28 (34), place dart marker, k to end of rnd.
NEXT (DEC) RND [K to dart marker, sl marker, ssk, k to 2 sts before next marker, k2tog, sl marker] twice, k to end of rnd—4 sts dec'd.

For sizes M (L, XL) only:
NEXT (SET-UP) RND K142 (151, 162), place dart marker, k37 (43, 46), place dart marker, k to end of rnd.
NEXT (DEC) RND K to dart marker, sl marker, ssk, k to 2 sts before next dart marker, k2tog, sl marker, k to end of rnd—2 sts dec'd.

summerdale dress

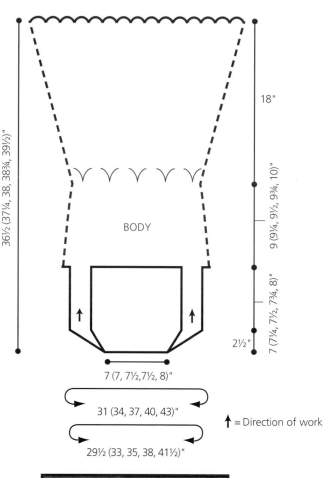

For all sizes:
Rep dec rnd every 10th rnd 2 (2, 5, 5, 5) times more—178 (198, 210, 230, 250) sts.
Work even in St st until body measures 9 (9¼, 9½, 9¾, 10)"/23 (23.5, 24, 24.5, 25)cm from underarm.

SKIRT
SET-UP RND *Kfb; rep from * to last 6 (6, 0, 0, 0) sts, k6 (6, 0, 0, 0)—350 (390, 420, 460, 500) sts.
Work pleated pattern until skirt measures 18"/45cm from waist, or desired length. Bind off using sewn bind-off method.

FINISHING
COLLAR
With larger needles, bind off 36 (44, 50, 58, 64) sts.
Work even in St st until piece measures 22 (22½, 23½, 24, 25)"/56 (57, 59.5, 61, 63.5)cm. Bind off loosely.
Sew cast-on and bound-off edges of collar piece to cast-on edge of front neckline, overlapping at center. Sew sides evenly along inner neckline selvedges and along back neck.

BELT
With smaller needles, cast on 15 sts.
Work in linen st for 22 (25, 28, 31, 34)"/56 (63.5, 71, 78.5, 86.5)cm, end with a WS row.
INC ROW (RS) K1, M1, *sl 1 wyif, k1; rep from * to last st, M1, k1—2 sts inc'd.
Rep inc row every other row 9 times more—35 sts.
Work even until belt measures 51 (57, 63, 69, 75)"/129.5 (144.5, 160, 175, 190.5)cm, end with a WS row.
DEC ROW (RS) K1, ssk, *sl 1 wyif, k1; rep from * to last 3 sts, k2tog, k1—2 sts dec'd.
Rep dec row every other row 9 times more—15 sts.
Work even until piece measures 73 (82, 91, 100, 109)"/185 (208, 231, 254, 276.5)cm, or desired length.
Belt should be long enough to go around waist twice and tie in front. Bind off in pat. ✳

36½ (37¼, 38, 38¾, 39½)"

18"

9 (9¼, 9½, 9¾, 10)"

7 (7¼, 7½, 7¾, 8)"

2½"

BODY

7 (7, 7½, 7½, 8)"

31 (34, 37, 40, 43)"

29½ (33, 35, 38, 41½)"

↑ = Direction of work

brandywine stole

DESIGNED BY
ANNIKEN ALLIS

A rectangular design of geometric lace and subtle texture is equally elegant worn as a neck-warming scarf or a shoulder-hugging stole.

FINISHED MEASUREMENTS
19 x 52"/48 x 132cm

YARN & NOTIONS
1 ball *Findley* in color #04 Renaissance

US 3 (3.25mm) straight needles *or size used to obtain gauge*

GAUGE
24 sts and 31 rows = 4"/10cm in chart pat with US 3 (3.25mm) needles.
Take time to check your gauge.

NOTE
To cast on loosely, hold 2 US 3 (3.25mm) needles tog and cast on sts around both needles at once. When cast-on is complete, withdraw 2nd needle and begin work as directed.

SHAWL
Cast on 116 sts loosely.

BORDER RIB
NEXT ROW (RS) K2, p4, *k5, p4; rep from * to last 2 sts, k2.
NEXT ROW K6, *p5, k4; rep from * to last 2 sts, k2.
Rep last 2 rows 4 times more for border rib.

BEGIN CHART
ROW 1 (RS) Work to rep line, work 18-st rep 6 times across, work to end of chart.
Cont to work chart in this way until row 32 is complete.
Rep rows 1–32 eleven times more. Piece measures approx 51"/129.5cm from beg.

brandywine stole

BORDER RIB

Work 10 rows border rib as for beginning.

Bind off as foll: K2, *sl 2 sts back to LH needle and k2tog tbl, k1; rep from * until all sts have been worked. Fasten off.

FINISHING

Block to measurements.✳

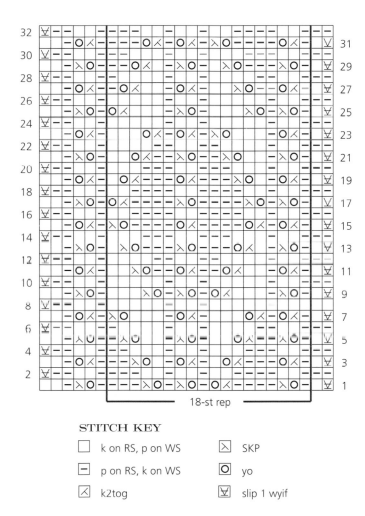

18-st rep

STITCH KEY

☐	k on RS, p on WS	⅄	SKP
─	p on RS, k on WS	◯	yo
⊼	k2tog	⊻	slip 1 wyif

paducah pullover

DESIGNED BY
BONNIE FRANZ
■■■▢

Dressed down with jeans
or dressed up with a
pencil skirt, a snuggly
cable-and-rib turtleneck
is a must-have for your
winter wardrobe.

SIZES
XS (S, M, L, XL)
Shown in S.

FINISHED MEASUREMENTS
BUST 32 (36, 40, 44, 48½)"/81
(91.5, 101.5, 111.5, 123)cm
LENGTH 24 (24½, 25, 26, 27)"/61
(62, 63.5, 66, 68.5)cm
UPPER ARM 13 (14, 15, 16, 17)"/33
(35.5, 38, 40.5, 43)cm

YARN & NOTIONS
8 (8, 9, 11, 12) hanks *Moonshine*
in color #10 Cotton Candy

US 6 (4mm) circular needle,
16"/41cm long, and straight needles
or size used to obtain gauge

Cable needle, two stitch markers,
four stitch holders

GAUGE
31 sts and 27 rows = 4"/10cm
in cable pat with size US 6
(4mm) needles.
Take time to check your gauge.

GLOSSARY
6-ST RC Sl 3 sts to cn, hold to *back*, k3, k3 from cn.

RIB PATTERN
(multiple of 4 sts)
ROW 1 (RS) K1, *p2, k2; rep from * to last 3 sts, end p2, k1.
ROW 2 P1, *k2, p2; rep from * to last 3 sts, end k2, p1.
Rep rows 1 and 2 for rib pat.

CABLE PATTERN
(multiple of 16 sts plus 10 plus 2)
ROW 1 (RS) K1, *p2, k6; rep from * to last 3 sts, end p2, k1.
ROW 2 P1, *k2, p6; rep from * to last 3 sts, end k2, p1.
ROW 3 K1, *p2, 6-st RC, p2, k6; rep from * to last 11 sts, end p2, 6-st RC, p2, k1.
ROW 4 Rep row 2.
ROW 5 Rep row 1.
ROW 6 Rep row 2.
ROW 7 K1, *p2, k6, p2, 6-st RC; rep from * to last 11 sts, end p2, k6, p2, k1.
ROW 8 Rep row 2.
Rep rows 1–8 for cable pat.

NOTES
1) When shaping on front and back, cross cables only when there is a sufficient number of sts.
2) Work incomplete cables in St st.

BACK
Cast on 124 (140, 156, 172, 188) sts. Work even in cable pat until piece measures 14 (14, 14, 14½, 15)"/35.5 (35.5, 35.5, 37, 38)cm from beg, end with a WS row.

SHAPE RAGLAN ARMHOLE
Bind off 11 (12, 13, 14, 15) sts at beg of next 2 rows—102 (116, 130, 144, 158) sts.
DEC ROW 1 (RS) K1, SKP, work in cable pat to last 3 sts, end k2tog, k1.
NEXT ROW K the knit sts and p the purl sts. Rep last 2 rows 30 (28, 26, 24, 20) times more.

paducah pullover

For sizes S (M, L, XL) only:
DEC ROW 2 (RS) K1, SKP, work in cable pat to last 3 sts, end k2tog, k1.
DEC ROW 3 (WS) P1, p2tog, work in cable pat to last 3 sts, end p2tog tbl, p1. Rep last 2 rows 3 (7, 11, 16) times more.

For all sizes:
Place rem 40 (42, 44, 46, 48) sts on st holder for back neck.

FRONT
Work as for back until armhole measures 6 (6½, 7, 7½, 8)"/15 (16.5, 18, 19, 20.5)cm, end with a WS row. Place marker (pm) to mark center 22 (24, 26, 28, 30) sts on the last WS row.

SHAPE NECK
Cont to shape raglan armholes as for back, work as foll:
NEXT ROW (RS) Work to center 22 (24, 26, 28, 30) sts, place these sts on st holder for front neck, join a 2nd ball of yarn, work to end. Working both sides at once, dec 1 st from each neck edge on next row, then every row 5 times more, then every other row twice. When all shaping is worked, fasten off 1 st each side.

SLEEVES
Cast on 64 (68, 68, 72, 72) sts. Work even in rib pat for 6 (8, 6, 4, 4) rows, end with a WS row.
NEXT (INC) ROW (RS) K1, M1, work in rib pat to last st, end M1, k1. Rep inc row every other row 0 (0, 0, 0, 7) times more, every 4th row 8 (18, 21, 23, 20) times, then every 6th row 8 (0, 0, 0, 0) times—98 (106, 112, 120, 128) sts. Work even until piece measures 17 (17, 17, 17½, 18)"/43 (43, 43, 44.5, 45.5)cm from beg, end with a WS row.

SHAPE RAGLAN CAP
Bind off 11 (12, 13, 14, 15) sts at beg of next 2 rows—76 (82, 86, 92, 98) sts.
DEC ROW 1 (RS) K1, SKP, work in rib pat to last 3 sts, end k2tog, k1.
NEXT ROW K the knit sts and p the purl sts. Rep last 2 rows 21 (22, 24, 24, 25) times more.
DEC ROW 2 (RS) K1, SKP, work in rib pat to last 3 sts, end k2tog, k1.
DEC ROW 3 (WS) P1, p2tog, work in rib pat to last 3 sts, end p2tog tbl, p1.
Rep last 2 rows 5 (6, 6, 7, 8) times more. Place rem 8 (8, 8, 10, 10) sts on holder.

FINISHING
Block pieces to measurements. Set raglan sleeves into raglan armholes. Sew side and sleeve seams.

TURTLENECK
With RS facing and circular needle, k 8 (8, 8, 10, 10) sts from left sleeve holder, pick up and k 19 sts evenly spaced along left neck edge, k 22 (24, 26, 28, 30) sts from front neck holder, pick up and k 19 sts evenly spaced along right neck edge, k 8 (8, 8, 10, 10) sts from right sleeve holder, then k 40 (42, 44, 46, 48) sts from back neck holder—116 (120, 124, 132, 136) sts. Join and pm for beg of rnds. Work around in k2, p2 rib for 6"/15cm. Bind off loosely in rib. ✳

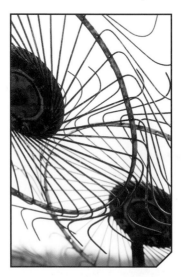

paducah pullover

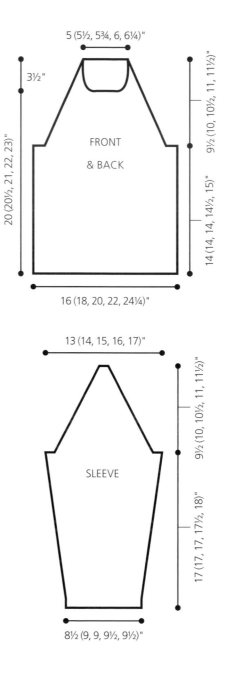

5 (5½, 5¾, 6, 6¼)"

3½"

FRONT
& BACK

9½ (10, 10½, 11, 11½)"

20 (20½, 21, 22, 23)"

14 (14, 14, 14½, 15)"

16 (18, 20, 22, 24¼)"

13 (14, 15, 16, 17)"

9½ (10, 10½, 11, 11½)"

SLEEVE

17 (17, 17, 17½, 18)"

8½ (9, 9, 9½, 9½)"

oak harbor pullover

DESIGNED BY
MARIE GRACE SMITH

In an organically elegant
design, a tweedy blend
of fibers complements
a leaf motif that circles the
yoke and is incorporated
into the sleeve edging.

SIZES
XS (S, M, L, 1X, 2X)
Shown in XS.

FINISHED MEASUREMENTS
BUST 32 (36, 40, 44, 48, 52)"/81
(91.5, 101.5, 111.5, 122, 132)cm
LENGTH 22¼ (22¾, 23¼, 24¼, 24¾,
25¼)"/56.5 (57.5, 59, 61.5, 63, 64)cm
UPPER ARM 11½ (13, 14, 15½, 16½,
18)"/29 (33, 35.5, 39.5, 42, 45.5)cm

YARN & NOTIONS
3 (3, 4, 4, 5, 5) hanks Sabine
in color #19 Biscuit

US 7 (4.5mm) circular needle,
29"/74cm) long, and double-pointed
needles *or size to obtain gauge*

Stitch markers, spare circular needle

GAUGE
19 sts and 30 rnds = 4"/10cm
in St st with US 7 (4.5mm) needle.
Take time to check your gauge.

GLOSSARY
LEAF MOTIF
(beg and end with 15 sts)
RND 1 K6, k3 wrapping yarn twice for each st, k6.
RND 2 K2tog, yo, k1, k3tog, slip each double-wrapped st,
dropping extra wraps from each st, then slip all 3 back to LH
needle, [k3tog but do not drop from needle, yo] 4 times, k3tog
once more and drop all from needle (9 sts made),
sssk, k1, yo, ssk.
RNDS 3, 5, 7, 9, AND 11 Knit.
RND 4 K1, k3tog, k3, yo, k3, yo, k3, sssk, k1.
RND 6 K2tog, yo, k2, k2tog, yo, k3, yo, ssk, k2, yo, ssk.

oak harbor pullover

RND 8 K2tog, yo, S2KP, yo, k1, yo, k3, yo, k1, yo, S2KP, yo, ssk.
RND 10 K1, k2tog, yo, k2tog, yo, k1, yo, S2KP, yo, k1, yo, ssk, yo, ssk, k1.
RND 12 K2tog, yo, k2tog, yo, k2, yo, S2KP, yo, k2, yo, ssk, yo, ssk.

BODY
Cast on 76 (86, 95, 105, 114, 124) sts, place marker (pm) for side, cast on 76 (86, 95, 105, 114, 124) sts, pm for beg of rnd—152 (172, 190, 210, 228, 248) sts. Join, being careful not to twist sts.
Work 16 rnds in garter st (k 1 rnd, p 1 rnd).
Knit 5 rnds.

SHAPE WAIST
NEXT (DEC) RND [K5, ssk, k to 7 sts before marker, k2tog, k5] twice—4 sts dec'd.
Cont in St st (k every rnd) and rep dec rnd every 6th rnd twice more—140 (160, 178, 198, 216, 236) sts.
Work even until piece measures 6"/15cm from beg.
Knit 5 rnds.
NEXT (INC) RND [K5, M1L, k to 5 sts before marker, M1R, k5] twice—4 sts inc'd.
Rep inc rnd every 6th rnd twice more—152 (172, 190, 210, 228, 248) sts.
Work even until piece measures 13½"/34.5cm.

SHAPE ARMHOLES
NEXT RND [K to 7 (7, 8, 9, 10, 10) sts before marker, bind off 14 (14, 16, 18, 20, 20) sts (discarding marker)] twice.
Leave sts on spare needle and set work aside.

SLEEVES
With dpns, cast on 45 (49, 55, 61, 65, 71) sts. Pm for beg of rnd and join, being careful not to twist sts.
SET-UP RND K15 (17, 20, 23, 25, 28), pm, k15, pm, k15 (17, 20, 23, 25, 28).
RND 1 P15 (17, 20, 23, 25, 28), sl marker, work rnd 1 of leaf motif over 15 sts, sl marker, p15 (17, 20, 23, 25, 28).
NEXT RND K15 (17, 20, 23, 25, 28), sl marker, work rnd 2 of leaf motif to next marker, sl marker, k15 (17, 20, 23, 25, 28).
Cont in garter st, working leaf motif between markers and garter st before and after, until rnd 12 is complete. Remove all but beg-of-rnd marker.
Knit 2 rnds.

SHAPE SLEEVE
NEXT (INC) RND K2, M1R, k to 2 sts before marker, M1L, k2—2 sts inc'd.
Cont in St st and rep inc rnd every 14 (12, 12, 12, 10, 10)th rnd 4 (5, 5, 5, 6, 6) times more—55 (61, 67, 73, 79, 85) sts.
Work even until sleeve measures 11½ (12, 12, 12½, 12½, 13)"/29 (30.5, 30.5, 32, 32, 33)cm from beg.
NEXT RND Work to 7 (7, 8, 9, 10, 10) sts before marker, bind off 14 (14, 16, 18, 20, 20) sts. Set aside. Make 2nd sleeve.

YOKE
Place all pieces on circular needle in the foll order: 1st sleeve, front, 2nd sleeve, back, pm for beg of rnd—206 (238, 260, 284, 306, 338) sts.
Knit 17 (21, 25, 29, 32, 36) rnds.
NEXT (DEC) RND [K16 (16, 50, 18, 49, 40), k2tog] 11 (13, 5, 14, 6, 8) times, k to end of rnd—195 (225, 255, 270, 300, 330) sts.

BEGIN LEAF MOTIF
NEXT RND Work rnd 1 of leaf motif 13 (15, 17, 18, 20, 22) times around.
Cont to work leaf motif in this way until rnd 12 is complete.
Knit 1 rnd.

oak harbor pullover

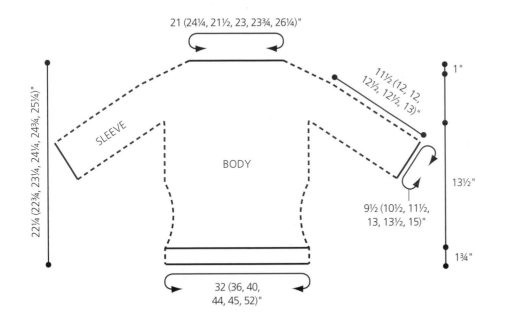

21 (24¼, 21½, 23, 23¾, 26¼)"

11½ (12, 12, 12½, 12½, 13)"

1"

22¼ (22¾, 23¾, 24¼, 24¾, 25¼)"

SLEEVE

BODY

9½ (10½, 11½, 13, 13½, 15)"

13½"

1¾"

32 (36, 40, 44, 45, 52)"

SHAPE NECK
NEXT (DEC) RND *K2, k2tog; rep from * to last 3 (1, 3, 2, 0, 2) sts, k to end—147 (169, 192, 203, 225, 248).
Knit 10 (11, 12, 14, 15, 16) rnds even.
NEXT (DEC) RND *K1, k2tog; rep from * to last 3 (1, 3, 2, 0, 2) sts, k to end—99 (113, 129, 136, 150, 166) sts.
Work 2 rnds even.
NEXT (DEC) RND *K0 (7, 4, 3, 2, 2), k2tog; rep from * to last 0 (5, 3, 1, 2, 2) sts, k to end—99 (101, 108, 109, 113, 125).
Work 10 rnds in garter st. Bind off loosely.

FINISHING
Sew underarm seams. Gently wash and block, taking care to block out leaf motifs and garter stitch borders. ✳

bedford shawl

DESIGNED BY
MARIE GRACE SMITH

Perhaps the perfect shawl:
a blend of modern short-row
shaping, a stockinette body
for warmth, and a pretty
picot and leaf-motif edging.

FINISHED MEASUREMENTS
WINGSPAN 67"/170cm
LENGTH AT CENTER Approx
16"/40.5cm

YARN & NOTIONS
3 hanks *Sabine* in color
#18 Clementine

US 7 (4.5mm) circular needle,
32"/80cm long, *or size used
to obtain gauge*

GAUGES
19 sts and 30 rows = 4"/10cm
in St st with US 7 (4.5mm) needle.

Leaf motif measures 3"/7.5cm
at widest point.
Take time to check your gauges.

GLOSSARY
LEAF MOTIF PATTERN
(beg and end with 15 sts)
ROW 1 (WS) P6, p3 wrapping yarn twice for each st, p6.
ROW 2 (RS) K2tog, yo, k1, k3tog, slip each double-wrapped st
dropping extra wraps, then slip all 3 back to LH needle,
[k3tog but do not drop from needle, yo] 4 times in same st,
k3tog in same st once more and drop from needle
(9 sts made), sssk, k1, yo, ssk.

bedford shawl

ROW 3 AND ALL WS ROWS Purl.
ROW 4 K1, k3tog, k3, yo, k3, yo, k3, sssk, k1.
ROW 6 K2tog, yo, k2, k2tog, yo, k3, yo, ssk, k2, yo, ssk.
ROW 8 K2tog, yo, S2KP, yo, k1, yo, k3, yo, k1, yo, S2KP, yo, ssk.
ROW 10 K1, k2tog, yo, k2tog, yo, k1, yo, S2KP, yo, k1, yo, ssk, yo, ssk, k1.
ROW 12 K2tog, yo, k2tog, yo, k2, yo, S2KP, yo, k2, yo, ssk, yo, ssk.

PICOT BIND-OFF
Bind off 2 sts, *sl first stitch on RH needle back to LH needle, cast on 2 sts, bind off 6 sts; rep from * until all sts are bound off.

NOTE
Shawl is worked in short rows; circular needle is used to accommodate large number of sts. Do not join.

SHAWL
Cast on 364 sts. Knit 8 rows.

BEGIN SHORT ROWS
NEXT ROW (RS) K186, turn.
NEXT ROW P8, turn.
NEXT ROW K12, turn.
NEXT ROW P16, turn.
Cont in this way, working 4 sts more in each short row, until all sts are worked, end with a WS row.
Knit 7 rows.
NEXT ROW (WS) K2, p to last 2 sts, k2.
NEXT ROW Knit.

BEGIN LEAF MOTIF PAT
NEXT ROW K2, work row 1 of leaf motif pat 24 times across, k2.
NEXT ROW K2, work row 2 of leaf motif pat 24 times across, k2.
Cont in this way, keeping first and last 2 sts of every row in garter st (k every row), until row 12 of leaf motif pat is complete. Purl 1 row.
Bind off using picot bind-off method.

FINISHING
Gently wash and block, taking care to pin out each picot point.✶

river falls cardigan

DESIGNED BY
SUSAN ADKINS
■■■▯

Femininity can be fabulous: a ribbon tie at the empire waist sets off a cascading lace bottom, echoed in the sleeves.

SIZES
S (M, L, XL)
Shown in S.

FINISHED MEASUREMENTS
BUST (CLOSED) 34 (37½, 41, 45)"/86 (95, 104, 114)cm
LENGTH 25½ (26, 26½, 27)"/65 (65, 67, 68.5)cm
UPPER ARM 12 (13¼, 13¾, 14¾)"/30.5 (33.5, 34, 37.5)cm

YARN & NOTIONS
4 (5, 5, 6) hanks *Zooey* in color #01 Sea Salt

US 4 (3.5 mm) circular needle, 40"/102 cm long, and straight needles *or size used to obtain gauge*

3yd/3m of ¼"/.65mm ribbon, stitch markers

GAUGES
22 sts and 28 rows = 4"/10cm in St st with size 4 (3.5mm) needles.

21 sts and 30 rows = 4"/10cm in chart pat with size 4 (3.5mm) needles.
Take time to check your gauges.

BACK
Cast on 93 (103, 113, 123) sts loosely. Knit 6 rows.

BEGIN CHART 1
ROW 1 (RS) K1 (selvage st), work to rep line, work the 10-st rep 9 (10, 11, 12) times across, sl 1 (selvage st).
ROW 2 AND ALL WS ROWS Purl to last st, sl 1 wyif.
Cont to foll chart in this way through row 10, rep rows 1–10 for 3 times more.

BEGIN CHART 2
ROW 1 (RS) K1 (selvage st), work to rep line, work the 10-st rep 8 (9, 10, 11) times across, work to end of chart, sl 1 (selvage st).
Cont to foll chart in this way, slipping last st of every row as established, through row 28, rep rows 1–28 once more.
Knit 1 row, purl 1 row.

EYELET EMPIRE WAISTBAND
DEC ROW 1 (RS) [K3, k2tog] 18 (20, 22, 24) times, k2, sl 1—75 (83, 91, 99) sts.
ROWS 2 AND 3 Knit.
ROW 4 Purl.
EYELET ROW 5 (RS) K1, *k2tog, yo; rep from *, end k1, sl 1.
ROW 6 Purl.
ROW 7 Knit.
ROW 8 Knit.
INC ROW 9 (RS) [K3, kfb] 18 (20, 22, 24) times, k2, sl 1—93 (103, 113, 123) sts.
Work in St st with selvage sts until piece measures 3"/7.5cm from eyelet band row 8.

SHAPE ARMHOLE
Bind off 3 (4, 4, 5) sts at beg of next 2 rows, 2 sts at beg of next 4 (4, 6, 8) rows.
DEC ROW (RS) K1, ssk, k to last 3 sts, k2tog, sl 1.
Rep dec row every other row 3 (5, 6, 7) times more—71 (75, 79, 81) sts.
Work even until armhole measures 6 (6½, 7, 7½)"/15 (16.5, 18, 19)cm.
Place markers to mark center 15 (15, 17, 19) sts.

river falls cardigan

SHAPE NECK
NEXT ROW K to marked sts, join a 2nd ball of yarn and bind off center 15 (15, 17, 19) sts, k to end.

Working both sides at once, bind off 4 sts from each neck edge once, 3 sts once, 2 sts once, and 1 st once—18 (20, 21, 21) sts rem each side. Work even until armhole measures 7½ (8, 8½, 9)"/19 (20.5, 21.5, 23)cm. Bind off rem sts each side.

LEFT FRONT
Cast on 53 (63, 63, 73) sts loosely. Knit 6 rows.

BEGIN CHART 1
ROW 1 (RS) K1 (selvage st), work to rep line, work 10-st rep 5 (6, 6, 7) times across, end sl 1 (selvage st).

ROW 2 AND ALL WS ROWS Purl to last st, sl 1 wyif.

Cont to foll chart in this way until row 10 is complete, rep rows 1–10 for 3 times more.

BEGIN CHART 2
ROW 1 (RS) K1 (selvage st), work to rep line, work the 10-st rep 4 (5, 5, 6) times across, work to end of chart, sl 1 (selvage st).

Cont to foll chart in this way, slipping last st of every row as established, through row 28, rep rows 1–28 once more. Knit 1 row, purl 1 row.

EYELET EMPIRE WAISTBAND
DEC ROW 1 (RS) [K5, k2tog] 7 (9, 9, 10) times, k3 (0, 0, 2), sl 1 (0, 0, 1)—46 (54, 54, 63) sts.

ROWS 2 AND 3 Knit.

ROW 4 Purl.

EYELET ROW 5 (RS) K1, *k2tog, yo; rep from *, end k0 (0, 0, 1), sl 1.

ROW 6 Purl.

ROW 7 Knit.

ROW 8 Knit.

INC ROW 9 (RS) [K5, kfb] 7 (9, 9, 10) times, k3 (0, 0, 2), sl 1 (0, 0, 1)—53 (63, 63, 73) sts.

Cont in St st, with selvage sts, until 5 (5, 11, 5) more rows are worked from inc row 9.

SHAPE NECK
NECK DEC ROW (RS) K to last 3 sts, k2tog, k1.

Rep neck dec row every other row 18 (23, 20, 29) times

more, then every 4th row 5 (5, 4, 1) times, AT THE SAME TIME, when piece measures same as back, shape armhole by binding off 3 (4, 4, 5) sts from armhole edge once, 2 sts 2 (2, 3, 4) times, then dec by k1, ssk at beg of foll 4 (6, 7, 8) RS rows—18 (20, 21, 21) sts. Work even until armhole measures same as back. Bind off.

RIGHT FRONT
Work as for left front, reversing shaping by working neck dec row as k1, SKP, k to end and armhole dec row as k to last 3 sts, k2tog, k1.

SLEEVES
Cast on 53 (63, 63, 73) sts loosely. Knit 6 rows.

BEGIN CHART 1
ROW 1 (RS) K1, work to rep line, work the 10-st rep 5 (6, 6, 7) times across, end sl 1 (selvage st). Cont to foll chart in this way through row 10. Rep rows 1–10 once more. Then, work in St st only, inc 1 st each side every 6th row 7 (5, 6, 4) times—67 (73, 75, 81) sts.

Work even until piece measures 10 (10, 10½, 11)"/25.5 (25.5, 26.5, 28)cm from beg.

SHAPE CAP
Bind off 3 (4, 4, 5) sts at beg of next 2 rows, 2 sts at beg of next 4 rows.

DEC ROW (RS) K1, ssk, k to last 3 sts, k2tog, sl 1.

Rep dec row every other row 20 (22, 23, 25) times more. Bind off 4 sts at beg of next 2 rows. Bind off rem 3 sts.

FINISHING
Block pieces to measurements. Sew shoulder seams.

FRONT AND NECK BORDERS
With circular needle, pick up and k 140 (146, 152, 156) sts to shoulder, 48 (48, 50, 52) sts across back neck, 140 (146, 152, 158) sts to lower edge. Knit 2 rows.

EYELET ROW (RS) K1, *k2tog, yo; rep from *, end k1. Purl 1 row. Knit 2 rows. Bind off knitwise. Set in sleeves. Sew side and sleeve seams. Weave ribbon through eyelet row in empire waistband. ✳

river falls cardigan

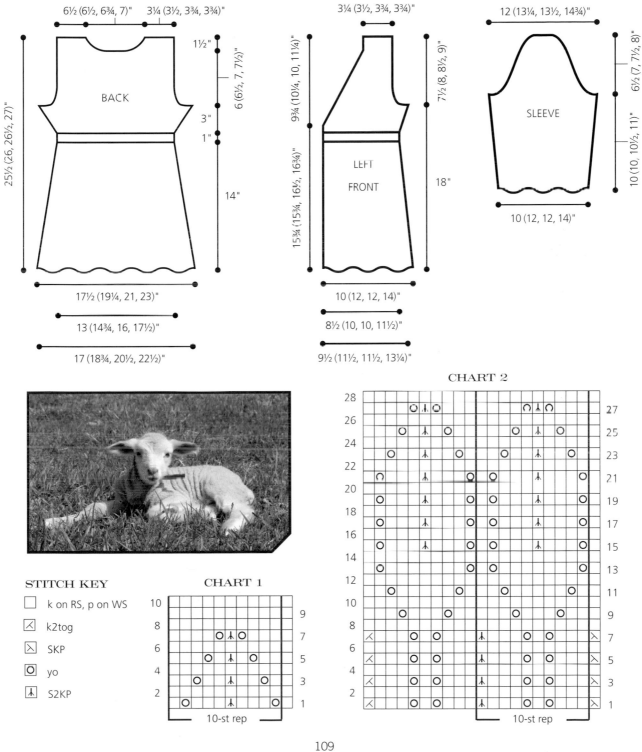

BACK

6½ (6½, 6¾, 7)"   3¼ (3½, 3¾, 3¾)"

1½"

6 (6½, 7, 7½)"

3"

1"

14"

25½ (26, 26½, 27)"

17½ (19¼, 21, 23)"

13 (14¾, 16, 17½)"

17 (18¾, 20½, 22½)"

LEFT FRONT

3¼ (3½, 3¾, 3¾)"

9¾ (10¼, 10, 11¼)"

7½ (8, 8½, 9)"

15¾ (15¾, 16½, 16¾)"

18"

10 (12, 12, 14)"

8½ (10, 10, 11½)"

9½ (11½, 11½, 13¼)"

SLEEVE

12 (13¼, 13½, 14¾)"

6½ (7, 7½, 8)"

10 (10, 10½, 11)"

10 (12, 12, 14)"

STITCH KEY

☐	k on RS, p on WS
⟋	k2tog
⟍	SKP
⍥	yo
木	S2KP

CHART 1

10-st rep

CHART 2

10-st rep

109

pella pullover

**DESIGNED BY
CAROLYN NOYES**
■■■▶

Two different weights of the
same yarn allow delicate
lace sleeves and side
panels to be anchored by a
stockinette front and back.

SIZES
S (M, L) Shown in S.

FINISHED MEASUREMENTS
BUST 33 (35, 37)"/84 (89, 94)cm
LENGTH 24 (24½, 25)"/61
(62, 63.5)cm
UPPER ARM 13½ (15, 15¾)"/34 (38, 40)cm

YARN & NOTIONS
5 (7, 8) balls *Findley DK* in color
#14 Bloom (A)
1 (1, 2) balls *Findley* in color
#12 Bloom (B)

US 5 (3.75mm) straight needles

US 4 (3.5mm) circular needle,
16"/40cm long *or sizes used to
obtain gauge*

Size G/6 (4mm) crochet hook,
stitch markers, one ⁷⁄₁₆" button

GAUGES
22 sts and 30 rows = 4"/10cm in St st
with US 5 (3.75 mm) needles and A.

18 sts and 30 rows = 4"/10cm
in lace pat st with US 5
(3.75 mm) needles and B.
Take time to check your gauges.

GLOSSARY
M1L (MAKE 1 INC LEFT) K into the back of the st (the purl
bump) in the row below the st on the RH needle.
M1R (MAKE 1 INC RIGHT) Insert LH needle into the back of the
st below st just worked and k this st.

LACE PATTERN
(multiple of 6 sts plus 1)
ROW 1 (RS) K1, *yo, ssk, k1, k2tog, yo, k1; rep from * to end.
ROWS 2, 4, AND 6 Purl.
ROW 3 K1, *k1, yo, S2KP, yo, k2; rep from * to end.
ROW 5 K1, *k2tog, yo, k1, yo, ssk, k1; rep from * to end.
ROW 7 K2tog, *yo, k3, yo, S2KP; rep from *, ending last rep
ssk (instead of S2KP).
ROW 8 Purl.
Rep rows 1–8 for lace pat.

NOTES
1) Back of sweater is worked in St st with A only. Front is
worked with side panels in lace st in B and center panel in A.
2) When changing from A to B on front, pick up new yarn
from under working yarn to avoid holes.
3) When working armhole displacement shaping in lace pat
with B, work added sts in St st until there are sufficient sts to
combine a dec with a yo to maintain increasing lace pat.
4) When working inc'd sts for sleeves in lace pat, markers
are used and inc's are worked on WS rows. Then inc'd sts
are worked in St st until a total of 6 sts are increased, so that
a complete pat can be worked. Lace pat st is worked across
these sts only after blocks of 6 inc'd sts are added.

BACK
With straight needles and A, cast on 96 (102, 108) sts.
[P 1 row, k 1 row] twice.
SET-UP ROW (RS) K22, place marker (pm), k52 (58, 64), pm, k22.
Cont in St st until piece measures 3½"/9cm from beg.

SHAPE BODY
DEC ROW (RS) K to marker, sl marker, ssk, k to 2 sts before next
marker, k2tog, sl marker, k to end.
Rep dec row every 4th row 7 times more—80 (96, 92). Work
even until piece measures 9"/23cm from beg.
INC ROW (RS) K to marker, sl marker, M1R, k to next marker,
M1L, sl marker, k to end.

pella pullover

Rep inc row every 10th row 4 times more—90 (96, 102) sts. Remove markers and work even until piece measures 16½"/42cm from beg.

SHAPE ARMHOLE
Bind off 4 sts at beg of next 2 rows, 2 sts at beg of next 2 (4, 6) rows—78 (80, 82) sts.
Work even until armhole measures 2¾ (3¼, 3¾)"/7 (8, 9.5)cm.

KEYHOLE OPENING
NEXT ROW (RS) K37 (38, 39), join a 2nd ball of yarn and bind off 4 sts, k to end. Working both sides at once, dec 1 st each side of neck edge on next 2 rows—35 (36, 37) sts rem each side. Work even until armhole measures 5½ (6, 6½)"/14 (15, 16.5)cm.
NEXT (INC) ROW (RS) K to last st of first side, M1L; on 2nd side, k2, M1R, k to end. Rep this inc row every RS row once more—37 (38, 39) sts each side. Work 1 row even.

SHAPE NECK
Bind off 9 sts from each neck edge once, then 8 sts once. Armhole measures 7 (7½, 8)"/18 (19, 20.5)cm.

SHAPE SHOULDER
Bind off 7 sts from each shoulder edge twice, then 6 (7, 8) sts once.

FRONT
With straight needles and A, cast on 100 (106, 112) sts. [P 1 row, k 1 row] twice. Cut A.

BEGIN PATTERNS
NEXT ROW (RS) With B, k18, pm; with A, k64 (70, 76), pm; with B, k18.
SET-UP ROW (WS) P2, p2tog, [p1, p2tog] 4 times, p2, sl marker, p to next marker, sl marker, p2, [p1, p2tog] 4 times, p2tog, p2—90 (96, 102) sts.
ROW 1 (RS) Work row 1 of lace pat over 13 sts with B, k64 (70, 76) with A, work row 1 of lace pat over 13 sts with B. Cont to work in this way until piece measures 3½"/9cm from beg.

SHAPE BODY
DEC ROW 1 (RS) Work lace pat with B to marker, sl marker, k1, ssk, k to 3 sts before next marker, k2tog, k1, sl marker, work lace pat with B to end.

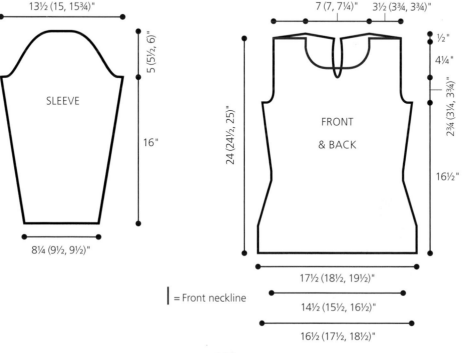

13½ (15, 15¾)"

5 (5½, 6)"

SLEEVE

16"

8¼ (9½, 9½)"

7 (7, 7¼)"   3½ (3¾, 3¾)"

½"

4¼"

2¾ (3¼, 3¾)"

16½"

24 (24½, 25)"

FRONT & BACK

17½ (18½, 19½)"

14½ (15½, 16½)"

16½ (17½, 18½)"

❘ = Front neckline

pella pullover

Rep dec row every 4th row 7 times more—74 (80, 86) sts. Work even until piece measures 9"/23cm from beg.

INC ROW (RS) Work lace pat with B to marker, sl marker, k2, M1R, k to 1 st before next marker, M1L, k1, sl marker, work lace pat with B to end.

Rep inc row every 10th row 4 times more—84 (90, 96) sts. Remove markers and work even until piece measures 16½"/42cm from beg.

SHAPE ARMHOLE

Bind off 4 sts at beg of next 2 rows, bind off 1 st at beg of next 2 rows—74 (80, 86) sts.

NOTE At this point, interior dec'ing will take place in St st section in A, with displacement adding of sts simultaneously in lace pat st in B. When adding sts in lace pat, work inc'd sts in St st until there are sufficient sts to work a dec with a corresponding yo.

DISPLACEMENT ROW (RS) K1, M1, work lace pat to marker, sl marker, k1, ssk, k to 3 sts before next marker, k2tog, k1, sl marker, work lace pat to last st, M1, k1. From this point on, work first and last st of every row in St st and work added sts into lace pat as described. Rep displacement row every other row 11 (12, 14) times more. There are 20 (21, 23) sts in each lace pat section, 34 (38, 40) sts in St st segment. Pm on last WS row to mark center 14 (14, 16) sts. At this point, displacement row will be discontinued and sts will be worked in pat throughout shaping of neck.

SHAPE NECK

NEXT ROW (RS) Work to marked center sts, join a 2nd ball of A and bind off these 14 (14, 16) sts, work to end. Working both sides at once, bind off 4 sts from each neck edge once, 3 sts once, 2 sts twice, and 1 st once—18 (21, 23) sts rem each side. When armhole measures same as back, bind off rem sts each side.

SLEEVES

With straight needles and A, cast on 44 (50, 50) sts. [P 1 row, k 1 row] twice. Cut A and cont with B only.

NEXT (DEC) ROW (RS) With B, knit, dec 7 sts evenly spaced—37 (43, 43) sts. P 1 row.

BEGIN LACE PAT

ROW 1 (RS) K1, work row 1 of 6-st rep 7 (8, 8) times across. Cont in lace pat until piece measures 3"/7.5cm from beg, end with a RS row.

INC ROW (WS) P1, M1 p-st, p to last st, M1 p-st, p1. Rep inc row every 4th row 11 (11, 13) times more—61 (67, 71) sts.

Work even until piece measures 16"/40.5cm from beg.

SHAPE CAP

Bind off 5 sts at beg of next 2 rows.

Dec 1 st each side of next row, then every other row twice more, then dec 1 st each side every 4th row once. Rep from * to * twice more. Then dec 1 st each side every other row 0 (3, 5) times more—27 sts rem.

Bind off 3 sts at beg of next 4 rows. Bind off 15 sts.

FINISHING

Sew shoulder seams. Set in sleeves. Sew side and sleeve seams.

NECKLINE TRIM

With circular needle, pick up and k 104 (104, 108) sts evenly around neck edge. K 1 row, p 1 row, k 1 row. Bind off, leaving last loop on needle. With crochet hook, ch 6, join to form button loop. Fasten off securely. Sew on button. Block finished piece lightly. ✳

quinby capelet

DESIGNED BY
MARIE GRACE SMITH
◖◼◻◗

Lace can be both delicate
and rustic, as in this
capelet that features
a cozy ribbed collar and
is knit in a tweedy
worsted-weight yarn.

SIZES
S (M, L, 1X)
Shown in S.

FINISHED MEASUREMENTS
WIDTH 30 (35, 42, 47)"/76 (89,
106.5, 109.5)cm
LENGTH FROM BACK NECK
16½"/42cm

YARN & NOTIONS
3 (4, 4, 5) hanks *Sabine*
in color #14 Muscadine

US 5 and 7 (3.75 and 4.5mm)
straight needles

US 5 (3.75mm) double-pointed
needles (set of 2) *or sizes used to
obtain gauge*

GAUGE
24 sts and 29 rows = 4"/10cm
in chart pat with larger needles.
Take time to check your gauge.

GLOSSARY
W3 [Sl 3 sts wyif, move yarn to back between needles, return sts to LH needle] twice, p3.

I-CORD
With 2 dpns, cast on 4 sts. *Knit one row. Without turning work, slide the sts back to the opposite end of needle to work next row from RS. Pull yarn tightly from the end of the row. Rep from * until desired length. Bind off.

SHAWL
With larger needle, cast on 179 (209, 249, 279) sts.
NEXT ROW (RS) K2, p2, work row 1 of chart to rep line, work 10-st rep 16 (19, 23, 26) times across, work to end of chart, p2, k2.
NEXT ROW (WS) P2, k2, work row 2 of chart to rep line, work 10-st rep 16 (19, 23, 26) times across, work to end of chart, k2, p2.
Cont to work in this way until row 12 is complete. Rep rows 1–12 until piece measures 16½"/42cm from beg, end with a row 12.
NEXT 2 ROWS Purl.
NEXT (EYELET) ROW (RS) K2, yo, k2tog, k2, yo, k2tog, *k3, yo k2tog; rep from * to last 6 sts, k2, k2tog, yo, k2.
NEXT 3 ROWS Purl.

COLLAR
Change to smaller needles.
NOTE RS of collar is WS of capelet when collar is turned down to wear.
NEXT ROW (RS) [P2, k2] twice, *p3, k2; rep from * to last 6 sts, p2, k2, p2.
NEXT ROW K the knit sts and p the purl sts as they appear for rib pat.
Work in rib pat for 4"/10cm or desired length of collar.
Bind off loosely.

FINISHING
Gently wash and block to measurements.
Make an I-cord approx 38"/96.5cm. Thread I-cord through eyelets and knot each end. ✳

quinby capelet

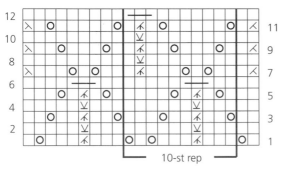

10-st rep

STITCH KEY

☐	k on RS, p on WS	⊼	k3tog
⟋	k2tog	⊞	W3
⟍	SKP	⎵	slip 1 wyib
⊙	yo		

meadow vale mitts

DESIGNED BY
ADRIENNE KU

The ideal accessory for spring and fall: a pair of lightweight mitts with a leaf lace pattern and a sweet ruffled edge at the cuffs.

SIZES
S/M (L)
Shown in S/M.

FINISHED MEASUREMENTS
HAND CIRCUMFERENCE
7 (8½)"/18 (21.5)cm
LENGTH 7½ (8)"/19 (20.5)cm

YARN & NOTIONS
1 ball *Findley* in color #29 Greengage

US 2 (2.75mm) double-pointed needles or size used to obtain gauge

Stitch markers, scrap yarn

GAUGE
30 sts and 48 rows = 4"/10cm after blocking in chart pat with US 2 (2.75mm) needles.
Take time to check your gauge.

GLOSSARY
K1, P1 RIB
RND 1 *K1, p1; rep from * around
RND 2 K the knit sts and p the purl sts.
Rep rnd 2 for k1, p1 rib.

MITT
CUFF
Cast on 84 (96) sts. Join, being careful not to twist sts, and place marker (pm) for beg of rnd.
Knit 2 rnds.
NEXT (RUFFLE) RND *[K2tog] twice, [kfb] 4 times, [ssk] twice; rep from * 6 (7) times more.
Knit 2 rnds.
NEXT (DEC) RND *[K2tog twice], k4, [ssk] twice; rep from * 6 (7) times more—56 (64) sts.
Knit 1 rnd, purl 1 rnd, knit 1 rnd.
NEXT (RIB) RND K1, *p2, k2; rep from * to 3 sts before end of rnd, p2, k1.
Rep rib rnd 19 times more.

119

meadow vale mitts

For size S/M only:
NEXT (DEC) RND K2tog, k26, k2tog, k to end of rnd—54 sts.

For size L only:
Knit 1 rnd.

For both sizes:
Purl 1 rnd, knit 1 rnd.

BEGIN CHART AND SHAPE THUMB GUSSET
NEXT RND K4, pm, work 10-st rep of rnd 1 for 5 (6) times around.
NEXT RND K to marker, sl marker, work 10-st rep of rnd 2 for 5 (6) times around.
NEXT (SET-UP) RND [Kfb] twice, k2, sl marker, work 10-st rep of chart 5 (6) times around—56 (66) sts.
NEXT 2 RNDS K to marker, sl marker, work 10-st rep of chart 5 (6) times around.
NEXT (INC) RND Kfb, k to 3 sts before marker, kfb, k2; sl marker, work to end of rnd—2 sts inc'd.
Cont to work chart in this way, rep inc rnd every 3rd rnd 8 (10) times more, AT THE SAME TIME, when rnd 16 of chart is complete, rep rnds 1–16 of chart until shaping is complete—74 (86) sts.
Work 2 rnds even in pat.
NEXT RND K1, place next 21 (25) sts on scrap yarn for thumb, cast on 1 st, work in pat to end of rnd—54 (64) sts.
Work 2 rnds even in pat as established.
NEXT (DEC) RND K2, k2tog, k to 1 st before end of rnd, sl 1 purlwise, remove marker, sl next st purlwise, k these 2 sts tog tbl, pm for new beg of rnd—52 (62) sts.
Work 1 row even.
NEXT (DEC) RND K2tog, k to 1 st before end of rnd, sl 1 purlwise, remove marker, sl next st purlwise, k these 2 sts tog tbl, pm for new beg of rnd—50 (60) sts.
Cont to work in chart pat as established for 10 (12) rnds more. Work 10 rnds in k1, p1 rib. Bind off.

THUMB
Pick up and k 1 st in cast-on st in thumb opening, k21 (25) from scrap yarn, pm for beg of rnd.
Knit 8 (10) rnds.
Work 4 rnds in k1, p1 rib. Bind off.✳

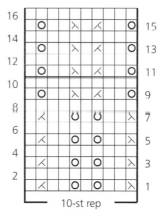

10-st rep

STITCH KEY

☐ knit

⊟ purl

◹ k2tog

◺ SKP

◉ yo

121

pebble creek pullover

DESIGNED BY
CAROLINE FRYAR
◼◼◼▭

A colorwork-yoke pullover
evokes Bohus style—knit
it in warm neutrals or
brighter tonal hues.

SIZES
XS (S, M, L, 1X) Shown in XS.

FINISHED MEASUREMENTS
BUST 34¼ (36½, 38¾, 41, 43½)"/
86 (91.5, 97, 103, 108.5)cm
LENGTH 24 (24¼, 24½, 24¾,
25)"/61 (61.5, 62, 63, 63.5)cm
UPPER ARM 12½ (13, 13½, 13¾,
14)"/31.5 (33, 34.5, 35, 35.5)cm

YARN & NOTIONS
8 (8, 9, 9, 10) hanks *Herriot* in color
#04 Walnut (MC)
1 hank each in colors
#08 Sycamore (CC1),
#07 Eucalyptus (CC2),
#06 River Birch (CC3), and
#05 Ghost Fern (CC4),

US 3 (3.25mm) circular needles,
24 and 16"/60 and 40cm long, and
double-pointed needles *or size used
to obtain gauge*

Stitch markers, stitch holders

GAUGES
22 sts and 28 rnds = 4"/10cm in St st
with US 3 (3.25mm) needle.

24 sts and 26 rnds = 4"/10cm
in chart pat with US 3
(3.25mm) needle.
Take time to check your gauges.

GLOSSARY
K2, P2 RIB
(multiple of 4 sts)
RND 1 *K2, p2, rep from * around.
Rep rnd 1 for k2, p2 rib.

SHORT ROW WRAP & TURN (W&T)
on RS row (on WS row)
1) Wyib (wyif), sl next st purlwise.
2) Move yarn between the needles to the front (back).
3) Sl the same st back to LH needle. Turn work. One st is
wrapped.
4) When working the wrapped st, insert RH needle under the
wrap and work it tog with the corresponding st on needle to
close or hide wrap.

SEWN BIND-OFF
1) Cut yarn, leaving a tail 3 times the circumference of the skirt
hem, and thread through tapestry needle.
2) Insert the needle purlwise through the first 2 sts on knitting
needle, and pull tight.
3) Insert tapestry needle knitwise into the first st and pull tight.
Drop st from knitting needle.
Rep steps 2 and 3 until all sts have been bound off.

BODY
With longer circular needle and MC, cast on 192 (204, 212,
224, 236) sts. Join, being careful not to twist sts, and place
marker (pm) for beg of rnd.
Work in k2, p2 rib until piece measures 5"/12.5cm from beg.
NEXT RND K96 (102, 106, 112, 118), pm for side, k to end of
rnd.
NEXT (DEC) RND [K1, k2tog, k to 3 sts before marker, ssk, k1]
twice—4 sts dec'd.
Cont in St st (k every rnd) and rep dec rnd every 3rd rnd 5
times more—168 (180, 188, 200, 212) sts.
Work even until piece measures 9"/23cm from beg.
NEXT (INC) RND [K1, M1, k to 1 st before marker, M1, k1]
twice—4 sts inc'd.
Rep inc rnd every 14th (14th, 10th, 10th, 10th) rnd 2 (2, 3, 3, 3)
more times—180 (192, 204, 216, 228) sts.
Work even until piece measures 14½ (14¾, 15, 15¼, 15½)"/37
(37.5, 38, 38.5, 39.5)cm. Set body aside.

pebble creek pullover

SLEEVE

With dpns and MC, cast on 48 (48, 52, 52, 52) sts. Join, being careful not to twist sts, and pm for beg of rnd. Work in k2, p2 rib until work measures 5"/12.5cm from beg.

SHAPE SLEEVE

NOTE Change to shorter circular needle when necessary.
NEXT (INC) RND K1, M1, k to last st, M1, k1—2 sts inc'd. Work in St st, rep inc rnd every 7th (7th, 8th, 7th, 7th) rnd 10 (11, 10, 11, 12) times more—70 (72, 74, 76, 78) sts. Work even until piece measures 16½ (17, 17, 17½, 18)"/42 (43, 43, 44.5, 45.5)cm, ending 3 (3, 3, 4, 5) sts before end of last rnd. Make 2nd sleeve.

YOKE

NEXT (JOINING) RND With MC, beg at beg-of-rnd marker on body (right underarm), k 3 (3, 3, 4, 5) sts and place them on st holder, pm, k to 3 (3, 3, 4, 5) sts before side marker, place next 6 (6, 6, 8, 10) sts on st holder, place 6 (6, 6, 8, 10) sts from first sleeve on holder, pm, k 64 (66, 68, 68, 68) sleeve sts, pm, k to last 3 (3, 3, 4, 5) body sts, placing these sts on st holder, place 6 (6, 6, 8, 10) sts from second sleeve on st holder, pm, k 64 (66, 68, 68, 68) sleeve sts. Pm for beg of rnd—296 (312, 328, 336, 344) sts.
NEXT RND With MC, knit, dec 2 (0, 4, 0, 2) sts evenly around—294 (312, 324, 336, 342) sts. Work 7 rnds in St st.

BEGIN CHART

RND 1 Work 6-st rep 49 (52, 54, 56, 57) times around. Cont to work chart in this way until rnd 36 is complete. Yoke measures approx 6½"/16.5cm—147 (156, 162, 168, 171) sts.

SHAPE NECK

Work short rows to shape back neck as foll:
SHORT ROW 1 (RS) K42 (45, 48, 50, 52), w&t.
SHORT ROW 2 (WS) P38 (41, 44, 46, 48), w&t.
SHORT ROW 3 (RS) K34 (37, 40, 42, 44), w&t.
SHORT ROW 4 (WS) P30 (33, 36, 38, 40), w&t.
SHORT ROW 5 (RS) K26 (29, 32, 34, 36), w&t.
SHORT ROW 6 (WS) P22 (25, 28, 30, 32), w&t.
NEXT RND K all sts, hiding wraps as you come to them.

NEXT (DEC) RND *K1, k2tog; rep from * around—98 (104, 108, 112, 114) sts.
NEXT RND Knit, dec 2 (0, 0, 0, 2) sts evenly around—96 (104, 108, 112, 112) sts.
Work in k2, p2 rib for 2"/5cm. Bind off loosely with sewn bind-off or another stretchy bind–off.

FINISHING

Graft underarms. Block to measurements. ✳

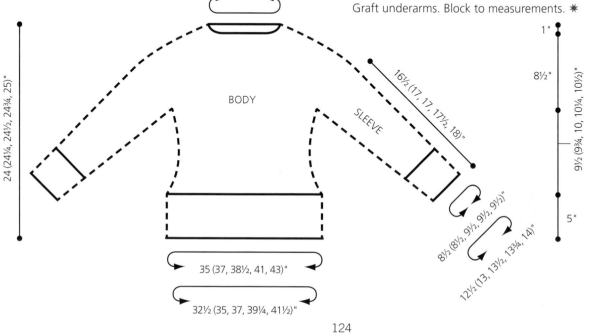

16¼ (17¼, 18, 18½, 19)"

BODY

SLEEVE

24 (24¼, 24½, 24¾, 25)"

16½ (17, 17, 17½, 18)"

1"

8½"

9½ (9¾, 10, 10¼, 10½)"

5"

35 (37, 38½, 41, 43)"

32½ (35, 37, 39¼, 41½)"

8½ (8½, 9½, 9½, 9½)"

12½ (13, 13½, 13¾, 14)"

COLOR & STITCH KEY

- ■ MC
- ■ CC1
- ■ CC2
- ■ CC3
- □ CC4
- ⊟ p
- ⊠ k2tog
- ⊼ S2KP

36

30

20

10

1

6-st
rep

rock springs wrap

DESIGNED BY
CRISTINA TUDOR

■■□▭

The unusual combination of mesh lace with color blocking creates a soft, modern piece whose subtlety is stunning.

FINISHED MEASUREMENTS
Approximately
18 x 60"/45.5 x 152.5cm

YARN & NOTIONS
1 ball *Zooey* each in colors #05 Cumin (A), #04 Taro (B), and #06 Sel Gris (C)

US 8 (5mm) straight needles *or size used to obtain gauge*

GAUGE
14 sts and 18 rows = 4"/10cm in lace pat after blocking, with US 8 (5mm) needles.
Take time to check your gauge.

LACE PATTERN
(over an odd number of sts)
ROW 1 (RS) K1, *yo, k2tog; rep from * to end.
ROW 2 Purl.
ROW 3 *K2tog, yo; rep from * to last stitch, k1.
ROW 4 Purl.
Rep rows 1–4 for lace pat.

NOTES
1) Work each color section with a separate ball of yarn; do not carry colors across work.
2) When changing colors, twist yarns on WS of work to prevent holes.
3) Divide C into 2 balls before beginning.

SHAWL
With A, cast on 12 sts; with B, cast on 38 sts; with C, cast on 13 sts—63 sts.
Work in lace pattern in colors as they appear for 77 rows. Break B.
NEXT ROW (WS) P12 with A, Join 2nd ball of C and p12, rejoin B and p26, p13 with C.
Cont in lace pat as established in colors as they appear for 126 rows more.
NEXT ROW (RS) Cont in lace pat, work 25 sts C, 14 sts B, 12 sts C, 12 sts A.
Cont in lace pat as established in colors as they appear for 23 rows more. Cut A.
NEXT ROW (RS) Cont in lace pat, work 25 sts C, 14 sts B, and 24 sts C.
Cont in lace pat as established in colors as they appear for 49 rows more.
Bind off on WS as foll: P2, sl 2 sts back to LH needle, p2tog, *p1, sl 2 sts back to LH needle, p2tog; rep from * until all sts have been worked. Fasten off.

FINISHING
To block, pin slightly larger than desired measurements, taking care to keep rows and stitches straight. Mist with water; or steam, being careful not to touch shawl with iron. Let dry completely before removing pins. ✱

ashland pullover

DESIGNED BY
MARIE GRACE SMITH
■■■▶

A geometric color pattern on a simply shaped crewneck is fun and fanciful.

SIZES
XS (S, M, L, 1X, 2X, 3X) Shown in XS.

FINISHED MEASUREMENTS
BUST 34½ (37½, 40¾, 43¾, 47, 50, 53¼)"/87.5 (95, 103.5, 111, 119.5, 127, 135)cm
LENGTH 22¼ (22½, 22¾, 23¼, 23¼, 23¼, 23¾)"/56.5 (57, 58, 59, 59, 59.5, 60.5)cm
UPPER ARM 17 (18, 18, 19, 20, 22¼, 23¼)"/43 (46, 46, 48.5, 51, 56.5, 59)cm

YARN & NOTIONS
6 (6, 7, 7, 8, 8, 9) balls *Tenzing* in color #05 Arctic River Blue (A)
5 (5, 5, 6, 6, 6, 7) balls *Tenzing* in color #03 Gingersnap (B)

US 5 (3.75mm) circular needles, 32 and 16"/80 and 40cm long, and double-pointed needles (set of 5)

US 6 (4mm) circular needle, 32"/80cm long, and double-pointed needles (set of 5) *or sizes used to obtain gauge*

Stitch markers, stitch holders, spare needle for 3-needle bind-off, scissors, sewing machine for steek

GAUGE
23 sts and 26 rows = 4"/10cm after blocking in chart pat with larger needles.
Take time to check your gauge.

GLOSSARY
K2, P2 RIB
(multiple of 4 sts)
RND 1 *K2, p2; rep from * around.
Rep rnd 1 for k2, p2 rib.

3-NEEDLE BIND-OFF
1) Hold right sides of pieces together on two needles. Insert third needle knitwise into first st of each needle, and wrap yarn knitwise.
2) Knit these two sts together and slip them off the needles. *Knit the next two sts together in the same manner.
3) Slip first st on 3rd needle over 2nd st and off needle. Rep from * in step 2 across row until all sts are bound off.

BODY
With smaller, longer circular needle and A, cast on 100 (108, 118, 126, 136, 144, 154) sts, place marker (pm) for side seam, cast on 100 (108, 118, 126, 136, 144, 154) sts, pm for beg of rnd—200 (216, 236, 252, 272, 288, 308) sts. Join, being careful not to twist sts.
Work in k2, p2 rib for 3"/7.5cm, dec 2 (0, 2, 0, 2, 0, 2) sts evenly in last rnd—198 (216, 234, 252, 270, 288, 306) sts. Change to larger needle.

BEGIN CHART
RND 1 Work 18-st rep of chart 11 (12, 13, 14, 15, 16, 17) times around. Cont in this way until rnd 14 is complete. Rep rnds 1–14 until piece measures 13¾ (13½, 13¾, 13¾, 13¼, 12½, 12¼)"/35 (34.5, 35, 35, 33.5, 32, 31)cm from beg.

SHAPE ARMHOLE
NOTE Work steek sts as [k1 A, k1 B] 3 times, k1A.
NEXT RND [Work to 8 (9, 10, 11, 11, 12, 13) sts before marker, bind off 16 (18, 20, 22, 22, 24, 26) sts for armhole] twice.
NEXT RND Cont in chart pat as established, cast on 7 steek sts over each set of bound-off armhole sts—180 (194, 208, 222, 240, 254, 268) sts. Pm for beg of rnd before first set of steek sts. Work even until armhole measures 5 (5½, 5½, 5¾, 6¼, 7¼, 8)"/12.5 (14, 14, 15.5, 16, 18.5, 20.5)cm.

SHAPE FRONT NECK
NEXT RND Cont in pat as established, k38 (41, 44, 48, 51, 54, 57), bind off 21 (22, 23, 22, 25, 26, 27) sts for front neck, k to end of rnd.

ashland pullover

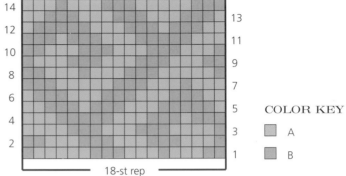

COLOR KEY

☐ A
☐ B

18-st rep

NEXT RND Cont in pat as established, k38 (41, 44, 48, 51, 54, 57), cast on 7 steek sts over bound-off sts. These 7 sts are neck steek sts and should be worked in alternating colors, as for armhole steek.

NEXT (DEC) RND Work to 2 sts before steek sts, k2tog, work steek sts, SKP—2 sts dec'd.

Rep dec rnd every other round 9 (9, 9, 10, 10, 10, 10) times more.

Work even on 146 (159, 172, 185, 200, 213, 226) sts until armholes measure 8½ (9, 9, 9½, 10, 11, 11½)"/21.5 (23, 23, 24, 25.5, 28, 29)cm.

NEXT RND Bind off 7 steek sts, place 21 (24, 27, 30, 33, 36, 39) shoulder sts on st holder, bind off 7 front neck steek sts, place 21 (24, 27, 30, 33, 36, 39) shoulder sts on st holder, bind off 7 armhole steek sts, place 21 (24, 27, 30, 33, 36, 39) shoulder sts on holder, place 41 (42, 43, 44, 47, 48, 49) back neck sts on holder. Turn work inside out, and join shoulders using 3-needle bind-off method.

SLEEVES

With smaller dpns, cast on 44 (48, 48, 52, 56, 60, 64) sts. Join, being careful not to twist sts, and pm for beg of rnd. Work in k2, p2 rib for 3"/7.5cm. Change to larger dpns.

BEGIN CHART

RND 1 Work 18-st rep of chart 2 (2, 2, 2, 3, 3, 3) times around, rep sts 1–8 (12, 12, 16, 2, 6, 10) once more.

SHAPE SLEEVES

Cont in chart pat as established, shape sleeves as foll, working new sts into chart pat:

Inc one st at beg and end of rnd every other rnd 14 (16, 14, 16, 18, 24, 26) times, then every 4th rnd 13 (12, 13, 14, 12, 10, 9) times—98 (104, 104, 110, 116, 128, 134) sts. Work even until sleeve measures 16½ (16½, 17, 17, 17, 17½, 17½)"/42 (42, 43, 43, 43, 44.5, 44.5)cm from beg. Bind off.

FINISHING

REINFORCE AND CUT STEEKS

With sewing machine, using a small stitch and loose tension, machine-stitch down one side of the center stitch, across the bottom and up the other side. With sharp scissors, cut along the center of the center stitch. ✳

COLLAR

With shorter, smaller needle and A, k 41 (42, 43, 44, 47, 48, 49) sts from back neck holder, pick up and k 67 (70, 69, 72, 69, 72, 71) sts evenly along front neck—108 (112, 112, 116, 116, 120, 120) sts.

Work in k2, p2 rib for 1½"/4cm.
Bind off loosely.
Sew in sleeves. Wash and block to measurements. ✳

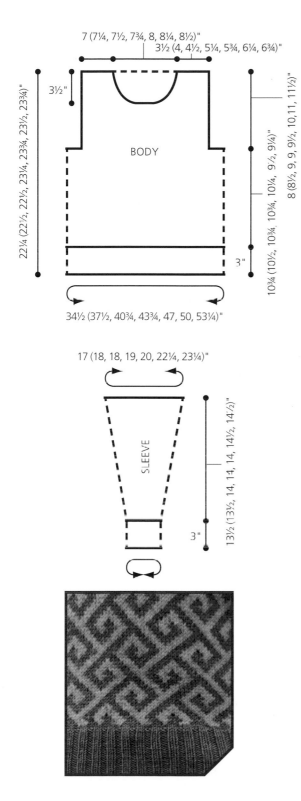

7 (7¼, 7½, 7¾, 8, 8¼, 8½)"

3½ (4, 4½, 5¼, 5¾, 6¼, 6¾)"

3½"

22¼ (22½, 22½, 23¼, 23¾, 23½, 23¾)"

BODY

8 (8½, 9, 9, 9½, 10,11, 11½)"

10¾ (10½, 10¾, 10¾, 9½, 9¼)"

3"

34½ (37½, 40¾, 43¾, 47, 50, 53¼)"

17 (18, 18, 19, 20, 22¼, 23¼)"

SLEEVE

13½ (13½, 14, 14, 14, 14½, 14½)"

3"

131

decorah cardigan

DESIGNED BY
ZAHRA JADE KNOTT
■■■■

Lace goes modern
with a diamond pattern
framed by geometric
ribbed panels that are
hemmed at the bottom
and cuffed at the sleeves.

SIZES
S (M, L, 1X)
Shown in S.

FINISHED MEASUREMENTS
BUST (CLOSED) 33 (38, 43¾ , 49)"/84
(96.5, 111, 124.5)cm
LENGTH 23 (24, 24½, 25)"/58.5 (61,
62, 63.5)cm
UPPER ARM 11½ (12½, 13½,
14½)"/29 (31.5, 34.5, 37)cm

YARN & NOTIONS
2 (3, 3, 3) hanks *Findley*
in color #18 Mermaid
3 (4, 4, 5) hanks *Findley DK*
in color #07 Mermaid

US 2 and 5 (2.75 and 3.75mm)
straight needles *or sizes used to
obtain gauge*

Crochet hook and scrap yarn
for provisional cast-on,
two ¾"/19mm buttons,
stitch markers

GAUGE
24 sts and 39 rows = 4"/10cm in
chart pat with larger needles and A.
Take time to check your gauge.

GLOSSARY
PROVISIONAL CAST-ON
Using scrap yarn and crochet hook, chain the number of sts to cast on, plus a few extra. Cut a tail and pull the tail through the last chain. With knitting needle and yarn, pick up and knit the stated number of sts through the "purl bumps" on the back of the chain. To remove scrap chain, when instructed, pull out the tail from the last crochet st. Gently and slowly pull on the tail to unravel the crochet sts, carefully placing each released knit st on a needle.

NOTE
When decreasing into chart pat, only work a yarn over with its paired decrease and vice versa; otherwise, work sts in St st.

BACK
Using larger needles and B, cast on 95 (111, 127, 143) sts using provisional cast-on method. Beg with a knit row, work 13 rows in St st (k on RS, p on WS), end with a RS row. Knit 1 row on WS for turning row. Cont in St st for 13 rows more, end with a RS row.
Remove provisional cast-on and carefully place 95 (111, 127, 143) sts from cast-on row on smaller needle. Fold work to WS along turning row and, with smaller needle, join hem as foll:
NEXT (JOINING) ROW (WS) *P next st from larger needle tog with next st from smaller needle; rep from * to end.
Change to A and cont with smaller needle. Work 2 rows in St st.

BEG CHART
ROW 1 (RS) Work chart to rep line, work 8-st rep 10 (12, 14, 16) times, work to end of chart.
Cont to work chart in this way through row 12, then work rows 1 and 2 once more.

SHAPE WAIST
DEC ROW (RS) K2, ssk, work in pat as established to last 4 sts, k2tog, k2.
Cont in chart pat as established, rep dec row every 10th row 4 times more—85 (101, 117, 133) sts. Work 16 rows even.
INC ROW (RS) K3, M1, work in pat to last 3 sts, M1, k3.
Cont in chart pat as established, rep inc row every 16th row 3 times more, working inc'd sts into pat—93 (109, 125, 141) sts. Work even until piece measures 15"/38cm from turning row, end with a WS row.

decorah cardigan

SHAPE ARMHOLE
DEC ROW (RS) K2, ssk, work in pat as established to last 4 sts, k2tog, k2.
Rep dec row every other row 4 (9, 14, 19) times more—83 (89, 95, 101) sts. Work even until armhole measures 7 (8, 8½, 9)"/18 (20.5, 21.5, 23)cm, end with a WS row.

SHAPE NECK AND SHOULDERS
Bind off 3 sts at beg of next 16 (16, 12, 8) rows, then 4 sts at beg of next 0 (0, 4, 8) rows, AT THE SAME TIME, join 2nd ball of yarn and bind off center 23 (29, 31, 33) sts, working both sides at once, bind off 2 sts from each neck edge twice, then dec 1 st at each neck edge every other row twice.

LEFT FRONT
With larger needles, cast on 47 (55, 63, 71) sts using provisional cast-on method. Work as for back to hem joining row. Change to A and cont with smaller needle. Work 2 rows in St st.

BEGIN CHART
ROW 1 (RS) Work chart to rep line, work 8-st rep 4 (5, 6, 7) times, work to end of chart.
Cont to work chart in this way through row 12, then work rows 1 and 2 once more.

SHAPE WAIST
DEC ROW (RS) K2, ssk, work in pat as established to end.
Cont in chart pat as established, rep dec row every 10th row 4 times more—42 (50, 58, 66) sts. Work 16 rows even.
INC ROW (RS) K3, M1, work in pat to end.
Cont in chart pat as established, rep inc row every 16th row 3 times more, working inc'd sts into pat—46 (54, 62, 70) sts. Work even until piece measures same as back to armhole, end with a WS row.

SHAPE ARMHOLE AND NECK
DEC ROW (RS) K2, ssk, work in pat as established to end.
Rep dec row every other row 4 (9, 14, 19) times more, AT THE SAME TIME, when armhole measures 3 (3½, 3½, 4)"/7.5 (9, 9, 10)cm, end with a WS row and work neck dec row as foll:
NECK DEC ROW (RS) Work in pat to last 4 sts, k2tog, k2.
Rep neck dec row every other row 16 (19, 20, 21) times—24 (24, 26, 28) sts when all shaping is complete.

Work even until armhole measures same as back to shoulder. Shape shoulder as for back.

RIGHT FRONT
Work as for left front, reversing all shaping.

RIGHT SLEEVE
With larger needles and B, cast on 52 (52, 60, 60) sts using provisional cast-on method. Beg with a knit row, work 21 rows in St st, end with a RS row. Knit 1 row on WS for turning row. Cont in St st for 21 rows more, end with a RS row. Remove provisional cast-on and carefully place 52 (52, 60, 60) sts from cast-on row on smaller needle. Fold work to WS along turning row and, with smaller needles, join hem as foll:
NEXT (JOINING) ROW (WS) [P next st from larger needle tog with next st from smaller needle] twice, pass 2nd st over first st on RH needle to bind off, cont in this way until 5 sts are bound off, then *p next st from larger needle tog with next st from smaller needle; rep from * to end—47 (47, 55, 55) sts.
Change to A and cont with smaller needles. Work 2 rows in St st.

BEGIN CHART PAT
ROW 1 (RS) Work chart to rep line, work chart rep 4 (4, 5, 5) times, work to end of chart.
Cont to work chart in this way for 2"/5cm, end with a WS row.
INC ROW (RS) K3, M1, work in pat to last 3 sts, M1, k3.
Rep inc row every 12th (10th, 10th, 8th) row 10 (13, 12, 15) times more, working inc'd sts into pat—69 (75, 81, 87) sts. Work even until sleeve measures 18 (18½, 19, 19)"/45.5 (47, 48, 48)cm from turning row, end with a WS row.

SHAPE CAP
Bind off 5 sts at beg of next 2 rows.
DEC ROW 1 (RS) K2, ssk, work in pat as established to last 4 sts, k2tog, k2.
Rep dec row 1 every other row 2 (2, 5, 7) times, then every 4th row 6 (8, 8, 8) times, then every other row 6 times. Work 1 WS row.
DEC ROW 2 (RS) K2, sssk, work to last 5 sts, k3tog, k2.
Rep dec row 2 every other row 5 times more. Work 1 WS row. Bind off rem 5 (7, 7, 9) sts.

decorah cardigan

LEFT SLEEVE
Work as for right sleeve to hem joining row. Omit bind-offs at beg of hem joining row. Bind off 5 sts at beg of foll RS row. Complete as for right sleeve.

SIDE PANELS (MAKE 2)
With smaller needles and B, cast on 13 sts.
\ROW 1 (RS) K1, *p1, k1; rep from * to end.
Cont in k1, p1 rib as established until piece measures approx 13½"/34.5cm, or length to fit along back side edge from hem joining row to armhole.

FINISHING
Block pieces to measurements. Sew shoulder seams. Sew side panels to back side edges and front side edges. Set in sleeves, centering underarm at center of side panel. Fold sleeve cuffs to RS along hem joining row, overlap cuff with bound-off edge behind. Sew buttons in place through all layers of overlapped cuff and sleeve near top of cuff.

NECK AND FRONT BAND
With smaller needles and B, cast on 13 sts. Work in rib as for side panels until piece fits along right front, neck, and left front edges, approx 56 (59, 60, 61)"/142 (150, 152.5, 155)cm. Sew neckband in place, adjusting length if necessary.✻

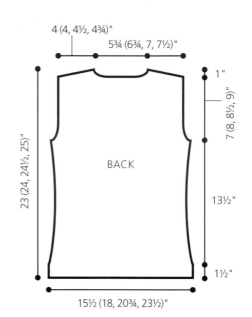

4 (4, 4½, 4¾)"
5¾ (6¾, 7, 7½)"
1"
7 (8, 8½, 9)"
23 (24, 24½, 25)"
BACK
13½"
1½"
15½ (18, 20¾, 23½)"

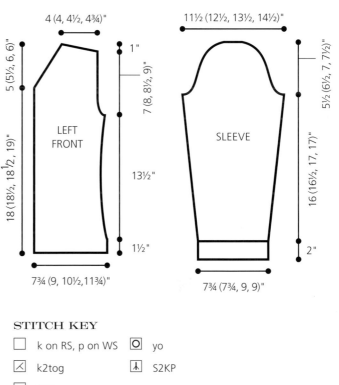

4 (4, 4½, 4¾)"
1"
5 (5½, 6, 6)"
7 (8, 8½, 9)"
18 (18½, 18½, 19)"
LEFT FRONT
13½"
1½"
7¾ (9, 10½, 11¾)"

11½ (12½, 13½, 14½)"
5½ (6½, 7, 7½)"
SLEEVE
16 (16½, 17, 17)"
2"
7¾ (7¾, 9, 9)"

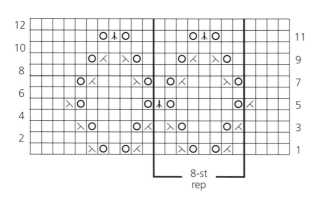

12
10
8
6
4
2
11
9
7
5
3
1
8-st rep

STITCH KEY
☐	k on RS, p on WS	◉	yo
⋌	k2tog	⅄	S2PK
⋋	SSK		

about the yarn

FINDLEY is our lace-weight yarn. You'll be glad it's in a ball, rather than a hank of 800 yards you have to wind! The yarn is smooth with a beautiful sheen. It's soft, doesn't split, and feels amazing knitted up.
> ✳ 3½oz/100g balls (each 798yd/730m); 50% merino wool/50% silk

FINDLEY DK is the DK version of our bestselling lace-weight blend.
> ✳ 1¾oz/50g balls (each 798yd/730m); 50% merino wool/50% silk

SABINE is my very favorite (don't tell the other yarns!) Why? It's a nice worsted weight, has a subtle tweediness, and is a year-round yarn in most of the world. Oh, and it's named after my dog, Sabine.
> ✳ 3½oz/100g hanks (each 218yd/199m); 40% cotton/30% merino wool/30% llama

MOONSHINE, a single-spun worsted-weight blend, is a dream to knit with. You'll love the depth of color and subtle variation the different fibers provide in both semi-solids and tonals.
> ✳ 3½oz/100g hanks (each 197yd/180m); 40% alpaca/40% wool/20% silk

ZOOEY is the quintessential summer yarn, with its slight thick-and-thin texture and DK weight. It softens substantially with washing—and it's machine washable.
> ✳ 3½oz/100g balls (each 284yd/260m); 60% cotton/40% linen

HERRIOT is named for literature's favorite veterinarian. This DK-weight yarn comes in 10 natural, undyed shades as well as 10 heathered shades. It's deliciously soft and utterly gorgeous!
> ✳ 3½oz/100g hanks (each 218yd/199m); 100% alpaca

HERRIOT GREAT is the chunky version of our wildly popular Herriot.
> ✳ 3½oz/100g hanks (each 131yd/120m); 100% alpaca

TENZING is a sport-weight yarn with a wonderfully soft hand and stitch definition that lends itself well to cables and colorwork.
> ✳ 1¾oz/50g balls (each 153yd/140m); 85% merino wool/15% yak

tips & tools

SKILL LEVELS

■☐☐☐

BEGINNER
Ideal first project.

■■☐☐

EASY
Basic stitches, minimal shaping, and simple finishing.

■■■☐

INTERMEDIATE
For knitters with some experience. More intricate stitches, shaping, and finishing.

■■■■

EXPERIENCED
For knitters able to work patterns with complicated shaping and finishing.

ABBREVIATIONS

approx	approximately
beg	begin(ning)
CC	contrasting color
ch	chain
cm	centimeter(s)
cn	cable needle
cont	continu(e)(ing)
dec	decreas(e)(ing)
dpn(s)	double-pointed needle(s)
foll	follow(s)(ing)
g	gram(s)
inc	increase(e)(ing)
k	knit
kfb	knit into the front and back of a stitch—one stitch has been increased
k2tog	knit 2 stitches together—one stitch has been decreased
LH	left-hand
lp(s)	loop(s)
m	meter(s)
mm	millimeter(s)
MC	main color
M1 or M1L	make one or make one left (see glossary)
M1 p-st	make one purl stitch (see glossary)
M1R	make one right (see glossary)
oz	ounce(s)
p	purl
pfb	purl into front and back of a stitch—one stitch has been increased
pat(s)	pattern(s)
pm	place marker
psso	pass slip stitch(es) over
p2tog	purl two stitches together—one stitch has been decreased
rem	remain(s)(ing)

rep	repeat
RH	right-hand
RS	right side(s)
rnd(s)	round(s)
SKP	slip 1, knit 1, pass slip stitch over—one stitch has been decreased
SK2P	slip 1, knit 2 together, pass slip stitch over the k2tog—two stitches decreased
S2KP	slip 2 stitches together, knit 1, pass 2 slip stitches over knit 1
sc	single crochet
sl	slip
sl st	slip stitch
spp	slip, purl, pass slip stitch over
ssk (ssp)	slip 2 sts knitwise one at a time, insert LH needle through fronts of sts and knit (purl) together
sssk	slip 3 sts one at a time knitwise, insert LH needle through fronts of sts and knit together
st(s)	stitch(es)
St st	stockinette stitch
tbl	through back loop(s)
tog	together
WS	wrong side(s)
wyib	with yarn in back
wyif	with yarn in front
yd(s)	yd(s)
yo	yarn over needle
*	repeat directions following * as indicated
[ ]	repeat directions inside brackets as indicated

glossary

BIND OFF Used to finish an edge or segment. Lift the first stitch over the second, the second over the third, etc. (U.K.: cast off)

BIND OFF IN RIB OR PAT Work in rib or pat as you bind off. (Knit the knit stitches, purl the purl stitches.)

CAST ON Place a foundation row of stitches upon the needle in order to begin knitting.

DECREASE Reduce the stitches in a row (for example, knit two together).

INCREASE Add stitches in a row (for example, knit in front and back of stitch).

KNITWISE Insert the needle into the stitch as if you were going to knit it.

MAKE ONE OR MAKE ONE LEFT Insert left-hand needle from front to back under the strand between last st worked and next st on left-hand needle. Knit into the back loop to twist the stitch.

MAKE ONE P-ST Insert needle from front to back under the strand between the last stitch worked and the next stitch on the left-hand needle. Purl into the back loop to twist the stitch.

MAKE ONE RIGHT Insert left-hand needle from back to front under the strand between the last stitch worked and the next stitch on left-hand needle. Knit into the front loop to twist the stitch.

NO STITCH On some charts, "no stitch" is indicated with shaded spaces where stitches have been decreased or not yet made. In such cases, work the stitches of the chart, skipping over the "no stitch" spaces.

PLACE MARKER Place or attach a loop of contrast yarn or purchased stitch marker as indicated.

PICK UP AND KNIT (PURL) Knit (or purl) into the loops along an edge.

PURLWISE Insert the needle into the stitch as if you were going to purl it.

SLIP, SLIP, KNIT Slip next two stitches knitwise, one at a time, to right-hand needle. Insert tip of left-hand needle into fronts of these stitches, from left to right. Knit them together. One stitch has been decreased.

SLIP, SLIP, SLIP, KNIT Slip next three stitches knitwise, one at a time, to right-hand needle. Insert tip of left-hand needle into fronts of these stitches, from left to right. Knit them together. Two stitches have been decreased

SLIP STITCH An unworked stitch made by passing a stitch from the left-hand to the right-hand needle as if to purl.

WORK EVEN Continue in pattern without increasing or decreasing. (U.K.: work straight)

YARN OVER Make a new stitch by wrapping the yarn over the right-hand needle. (U.K.: yfwd, yon, yrn)

KNITTING NEEDLES			
U.S.	METRIC	U.S.	METRIC
0	2mm	9	5.5mm
1	2.25mm	10	6mm
2	2.75mm	10½	6.5mm
3	3.25mm	11	8mm
4	3.5mm	13	9mm
5	3.75mm	15	10mm
6	4mm	17	12.75mm
7	4.5mm	19	15mm
8	5mm	35	19mm

rock springs wrap 126

gauge

Make a test swatch at least 4"/10cm square. If the number of stitches and rows does not correspond to the gauge given, you must change the needle size. An easy rule to follow is: To get fewer stitches to the inch/cm, use a larger needle; to get more stitches to the inch/cm, use a smaller needle. Continue to try different needle sizes until you get the same number of stitches in the gauge.

STANDARD YARN WEIGHTS TABLE

Categories of yarn, gauge range, and recommended needle and hook sizes

Yarn Weight Symbol & Category Names	**0** Lace	**1** Super Fine	**2** Fine	**3** Light	**4** Medium	**5** Bulky	**6** Super Bulky
Type of Yarns in Category	Fingering 10 count crochet thread	Sock, Fingering, Baby	Sport, Baby	DK, Light Worsted	Worsted, Afghan, Aran	Chunky, Craft, Rug	Bulky, Roving
Knit Gauge Range* in Stockinette Stitch to 4 inches	33–40** sts	27–32 sts	23–26 sts	21–24 sts	16–20 sts	12–15 sts	6–11 sts
Recommended Needle in Metric Size Range	1.5–2.25 mm	2.25–3.25 mm	3.25–3.75 mm	3.75–4.5 mm	4.5–5.5 mm	5.5–8 mm	8 mm and larger
Recommended Needle U.S. Size Range	000 to 1	1 to 3	3 to 5	5 to 7	7 to 9	9 to 11	11 and larger
Crochet Gauge* Ranges in Single Crochet to 4 inch	32–42 double crochets**	21–32 sts	16–20 sts	12–17 sts	11–14 sts	8–11 sts	5–9 sts
Recommended Hook in Metric Size Range	Steel*** 1.6–1.4mm Regular hook 2.25 mm	2.25–3.5 mm	3.5–4.5 mm	4.5–5.5 mm	5.5–6.5 mm	6.5–9 mm	9 mm and larger
Recommended Hook U.S. Size Range	Steel*** 6, 7, 8 Regular hook B–1	B–1 to E–4	E–4 to 7	7 to I–9	I–9 to K–10½	K–10½ to M–13	M–13 and larger

* Guidelines only: The above reflect the most commonly used gauges and needle or hook sizes for specific yarn categories.
** Lace weight yarns are usually knitted or crocheted on larger needles and hooks to create lacy, open-work patterns. Accordingly, a gauge range is difficult to determine. Always follow the gauge stated in your pattern.
*** Steel crochet hooks are sized differently from regular hooks—the higher the number, the smaller the hook, which is the reverse of regular hook sizing.

metric conversions

To convert from inches to centimeters, simply multiply by 2.54.

dyer brook blouse 14

techniques

KITCHENER STITCH (GRAFTING)

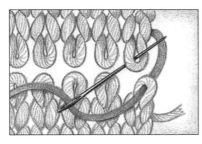

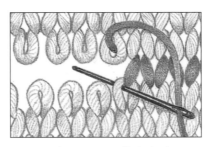

PROVISIONAL CAST-ON

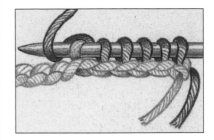

1. Insert the yarn needle purlwise into the first stitch on the front piece, then knitwise into the first stitch on the back piece.

2. Insert the yarn needle knitwise into the first stitch on the front piece again. Draw the yarn through.

With scrap yarn, make a crochet chain a few stitches longer than the number of stitches to be cast on. With main yarn, pick up one stitch in the back loop of each chain. To knit from the cast-on edge, carefully unpick the chain, placing the live stitches one by one on a needle.

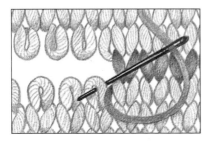

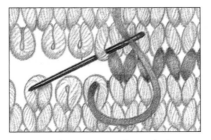

3. Insert the yarn needle purlwise into the next stitch on the front piece. Draw the yarn through.

4. Insert the yarn needle purlwise into the first stitch on the back piece again. Draw the yarn through.

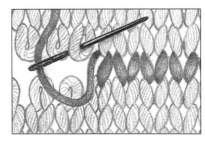

pebble creek pullover 122

5. Insert the yarn needle knitwise into the next stitch on the back piece. Draw the yarn through. Repeat steps 2 through 5.

acknowledgments

When you sit down to work on your first book, the first thing you figure out is that you have absolutely no idea what you are doing.

If you are very lucky, your publisher is Sixth&Spring Books/Soho Publishing. Everyone there knows exactly what they are doing. They were incredibly patient and kind but also pushed me to do better work. I am so very grateful to each of you for your help.

Soho's Trisha Malcolm has impeccable taste and amazing tact, and she has gently steered me in the right direction more times than I can count.

I was also fortunate to work with a dream team of designers on this book. Thanks to each of them for their lovely contribution.

Enormous thanks to our models for braving the Polar Vortex in delicate knitwear and doing it with smiles on their faces. You are pros!

Michelle Lukezic helped me with the post-processing of many of the images. I don't know what I did in a past life to deserve such an amazingly talented graphic designer, but I'm glad I did it!

I owe so much to so many friends for pitching in. Tanya Brooks and Cris Ferguson rearranged their families' schedules and used vacation time to lend a hand at the photo shoots. Lauria Kincaid kept the trains running on time. The entire Karasz clan let us take over their house and their lives. Christopher DeGasperi provided hot and cold running lambs and a beautiful bank barn to shoot in. Kristin McCurry and Charlie Cadigan let me run a B&B out of their basement. And Jeannie Bloch encouraged me to stand up for my vision and make sure this book reflected my own aesthetic.

Jen Fariello and Robert Radifera, my photography mentors, were both generous with their time and their studios. They taught me everything I know about taking pictures.

Finally, I want to thank the Juniper Moon Farm Aunties. It's much easier to step outside your comfort zone when you have a team of cheerleaders behind you. You all have been with me for every step of this journey, and I am ever humbled by your support.

index

a

abbreviations 139
Abilene Stole 10–13
Ashland Pullover 128–131

b

Bedford Shawl 101–103
Brandywine Stole 89–91

c

cable projects
  Cody Hat and Cowl 38–41
  Edgewater Shawl 56–59
  Hopewell Hat and Mitts 76–81
  Mattatuck Tee 20–23
  Paducah Pullover 92–96
  Pebble Creek Pullover 122–125
  Williston Hat 66–68
Carroll Cardigan 42–47
Cloudcroft Pullover 82–84
Cody Hat and Cowl 38–41
colorwork projects
  Ashland Pullover 128–131
  County Line Vest 72–75
  Darlington Dress 27–31
  Maryville Cardigan 60–65
  Williston Hat 66–68
County Line Vest 72–75

d

Darlington Dress 27–31
Decorah Cardigan 132–137
Dyer Brook Blouse 14–19

e

Edgewater Shawl 56–59

f

Fayette Stole 48–50

g

gauge 141
glossary 140

h

Hopewell Hat and Mitts 76–81

k

Kitchener stitch 142
knitting needle sizes 140

l

lace projects
  Abilene Stole 10–13
  Bedford Shawl 101–103
  Brandywine Stole 89–91
  Carroll Cardigan 42–47
  Decorah Cardigan 132–137
  Dyer Brook Blouse 14–19
  Fayette Stole 48–50
  Meadow Vale Mitts 119–121
  Oak Harbor Pullover 97–100
  Pella Pullover 110–115
  Quinby Capelet 116–118
  River Falls Cardigan 104–109
  Rock Springs Wrap 126–127
  Silverton Top and Cowl 32–37
  Traverse City Tunic 51–55

m

Maryville Cardigan 60–65
Mattatuck Tee 20–23
Meadow Vale Mitts 119–121
metric conversions 141

o

Oak Harbor Pullover 97–100

p

Paducah Pullover 92–96
Pebble Creek Pullover 122–125
Pella Pullover 110–115
provisional cast-on 142

q

Quinby Capelet 116–118

r

River Falls Cardigan 104–109
Rock Springs Wrap 126–127

s

Sheridan Shawl 24–26
Silverton Top and Cowl 32–37
skill level key 139
Spring Hill Scarf 69–71
standard yarn weights 141
Summerdale Dress 85–88

t

tools 139–142
Traverse City Tunic 51–55

w

Williston Hat 66–68

y

yarn information 138